OCR
TEXT PROCESSING
(BUSINESS PROFESSIONAL)

LEVEL 2 BOOK 1

OCR RECOGNISING ACHIEVEMENT | HODDER EDUCATION

Official Publisher Partnership

OCR
TEXT PROCESSING
(BUSINESS PROFESSIONAL)
LEVEL 2 BOOK **1**

TEXT PRODUCTION, WORD PROCESSING AND AUDIO TRANSCRIPTION

EDITOR: JILL DOWSON

ROSALIND BUXTON • LESLEY DAKIN • BEVERLY LORAM
• JANE QUIBELL • JEAN RAY • PAM SMITH • SARAH WAREING

HODDER EDUCATION
AN HACHETTE UK COMPANY

Orders: please contact Bookpoint Ltd, 130 Milton Park, Abingdon, Oxon OX14 4SB.
Telephone: +44 (0)1235 827720. Fax: +44 (0)1235 400454. Lines are open from 9.00am to 5.00pm,
Monday to Saturday, with a 24-hour message-answering service. You can also order through our website
www.hoddereducation.co.uk

If you have any comments to make about this, or any of our other titles, please send them to
educationenquiries@hodder.co.uk

British Library Cataloguing in Publication Data
A catalogue record for this title is available from the British Library

ISBN: 978 0 340 99185 5

First Edition Published 2009
Impression number   10 9 8 7 6 5 4 3 2 1
Year   2013 2012 2011 2010 2009

Hachette UK's policy is to use papers that are natural, renewable and recyclable products and made from
wood grown in sustainable forests. The logging and manufacturing processes are expected to conform to
the environmental regulations of the country of origin.

Cover photo © Influx Productions
Typeset by Dorchester Typesetting Group Ltd
Printed in Malta for Hodder Education, an Hachette UK company, 338 Euston Road, London NW1 3BH

CONTENTS

5 WORKED EXAMPLES — 183

THE AUTHORS

The following authors, who have provided all the material for this book, are Chief Examiners/Examiners for the Oxford, Cambridge and RSA Examination Board: Rosalind Buxton, Lesley Dakin, Beverly Loram, Jane Quibell, Jean Ray, Pam Smith and Sarah Wareing. The Series Editor is Jill Dowson.

TEXT PROCESSING (BUSINESS PROFESSIONAL) SUITE PUBLISHED BY HODDER EDUCATION, ENDORSED BY OCR EXAMINATION BOARD

Level 1 – Book 1 Text Production – core unit Word Processing Audio-Transcription	Level 1 – Book 2 Mailmerge Business Presentations Legal Text Processing
Level 2 – Book 1* Text Production – core unit Word Processing Audio-Transcription	Level 2 – Book 2 Medical Word Processing Medical Audio-Transcription Legal Audio-Transcription
Level 2 – Book 3 Mailmerge Business Presentations Document Presentation	
Level 3 – Book 1 Text Production – core unit Word Processing Audio-Transcription	Level 3 – Book 2 Legal Word Processing Document Presentation

* Level 2 – Book 1 is the first book in the series to be published. It will be closely followed by Level 1 – Book 1 and Level 3 – Book 1. Material covering the other units is planned for 2010.

INTRODUCTION

About the book

This series of textbooks is designed to help you build on the knowledge and skills you have already acquired so that you can progress to more advanced and varied text processing work in order to gain an Award, Certificate and Diploma in Text Processing (Business Professional).

It presumes that you already have a basic knowledge of the keyboard and how to use Microsoft® Word, or similar software, to produce basic documents.

This book contains the background information, practice exercises and practice exams you require to prepare for the OCR Text Processing (Business Professional) exam units in:

- Text Production Level 2
- Word Processing Level 2
- Audio-Transcription Level 2.

The book is divided into the following chapters.

- **Introduction:** this covers the contents of the book, together with an overview of the Text Processing (Business Professional) suite of qualifications at Level 2.
- **Assessment Criteria:** this chapter contains the syllabuses, or unit contents, for the three units. Each syllabus lists the items you will be tested on in the exams, and the relevant knowledge, understanding and skills that you need to acquire in order to complete these exams. It also gives details of the marking schemes, complete with tutors' notes, so that you can see exactly how your exam paper will be marked.
- **Knowledge, Understanding and Skills:** this chapter provides detailed notes, together with exercises that enable you to practise the skills you need to master before attempting a full practice exam for each unit. Following each set of notes, there are three examples of each type of document. Templates, recall text, graphics and dictation are available on the Hodder Plus website at: **www.hodderplus.co.uk/ocrtextprocessing**.
- **Exam Work:** this chapter provides hints for exam work, together with three new practice exams similar to the OCR standard for each unit. Templates, recall text, graphics and dictation are available on the Hodder Plus website at: **www.hodderplus.co.uk/ocrtextprocessing.**
- **Worked Examples:** printouts of correct worked examples of all practice exercises and exams are supplied in this chapter. Note that each of these shows only one way of displaying the documents – for example, your method of emphasis may not be the same, your line ends may differ slightly

or you may have left extra linespacing after headings. This is acceptable, as long as you have followed instructions and formatted your document consistently.

The Text Processing (Business Professional) suite of qualifications

Overview of Level 2

The Text Processing suite of qualifications has been designed to assess candidates' ability to produce a range of relevant and straightforward business documents, to meet the requirements of employment. The units that make up this qualification are drawn directly from the RSA Text Processing Modular Awards Stage II, which are widely recognised by employers as the benchmark qualifications in text processing.

The qualifications are nationally accredited onto the Qualifications and Credit Framework (QCF).

These qualifications are suitable for candidates who:

- have sufficient skill, underpinning knowledge and command of English to carry out the production of business documents without supervision
- are following programmes of study in administration at Level 2
- are already employed in text processing or administrative job roles, and wish to further develop their knowledge and expertise in this area.

Qualification structures

Candidates enter each unit separately and a unit certificate will be issued. On achievement of each unit the candidate will be awarded a number of credits. If a candidate wishes to achieve a Text Processing (Business Professional) Award, Certificate or Diploma, credits will need to be accumulated as described in the box below.

OCR Text Processing (Business Professional) Level 2 Award – 06958 (English)/04608 (Welsh)

The full OCR Level 2 Award in Text Processing (Business Professional) is awarded when the candidate has successfully completed **units to the value of at least nine credits**.

- Five of these credits must come from the Level 2 core unit, Text Production, in English, Welsh or the Screen Reader version. (The content is the same for each version of this unit, therefore candidates may choose only one.)

- The remaining four credits can be taken from the optional units at either Level 2 or 3.
- In order to receive the Award in Welsh, a candidate should be entered under scheme code 04608 and must take unit 03948 or 04606 to make up their optional credits.

*Please note that some combinations of units are barred – for full details of rules of combination, candidates should refer to their centres or access the OCR website on **www.ocr.org.uk**.*

OCR Text Processing (Business Professional) Level 2 Certificate – 06959

The full OCR Level 2 Certificate in Text Processing (Business Professional) is awarded when the candidate has successfully completed **units to the value of at least 16 credits**.

- Five of these credits must come from the Level 2 core unit, Text Production, in English, Welsh or the Screen Reader version. (The content is the same for each version of this unit, therefore candidates may choose only one.)
- Of the remaining credits, a minimum of five must be taken from the Level 2 or 3 optional units.
- Further credits required may be taken from the Entry Level or Level 1 optional units.

*Please note that some combinations of units are barred – for full details of rules of combination, candidates should refer to their centres or access the OCR website on **www.ocr.org.uk**.*

OCR Text Processing (Business Professional) Level 2 Diploma – 06960
The full OCR Level 2 Diploma in Text Processing (Business Professional) is awarded when the candidate has successfully completed **units to the value of at least 37 credits**. For the current versions of unit content, candidates and centres should refer to the Text Processing page of the OCR website.

- Five of these credits must come from the Level 2 core unit, Text Production, in English, Welsh or the Screen Reader version. (The content is the same for each version of this unit, therefore candidates may choose only one.)

- Of the remaining credits, a minimum of 18 must be taken from the Level 2 or 3 optional units.
- Further credits required may be taken from the Entry Level or Level 1 optional units.

Please note that some combinations of units are barred – for full details of rules of combination, candidates should refer to their centres or access the OCR website on www.ocr.org.uk.

The credits attached to the units achieved within each qualification are banked and may then contribute to the next qualification at the same level (e.g. if a candidate has achieved the required credit for the Level 2 Award, this credit can also be carried forward to the Level 2 Certificate).

Due to the flexible nature of qualifications within the QCF, these banked credits may also contribute to a higher qualification at a later stage of the candidate's progress.

Form of assessment

Each unit within these qualifications is assessed via an OCR-set and marked examination. Candidates will be required to carry out all assessment tasks within a stated error tolerance.

Results will be graded Distinction, Pass or Fail, depending upon the number of faults incurred, with the exception of the Shorthand Speed Skills and Speed Keying units, which will state the words per minute speed achieved on the certificate.

Units

Details of the unit contents for Text Processing, Word Processing and Audio-Transcription at Level 2 are provided in this book.

The flexibility of qualifications within the QCF means that candidates may take units at a higher or lower level than the level of their full qualification. For details of percentages allowed, candidates should refer to their centres or to the OCR website.

Group 1: core units

06975	Text Production – English	5 credits
03947	Cynhyrchu Testun	5 credits
00005	Text Production – Screen Reader	5 credits

Group 2: optional units

Level 2 Text Processing units

06976	Audio-Transcription	4 credits
06977	Business Presentations	5 credits
06978	Document Presentation	5 credits
06980	Legal Audio-Transcription	5 credits
06994	Mailmerge	5 credits
06995	Medical Audio-Transcription	5 credits
06996	Medical Word Processing	5 credits
06997	Shorthand Speed Skills	5 credits
06998	Speed Keying	4 credits
06999	Word Processing – English	5 credits
03948	Prosesu Geiriau	5 credits

Level 3 Text Processing units

03933	Audio-Transcription	5 credits
03934	Document Presentation	6 credits
03935	Legal Word Processing	6 credits
03936	Shorthand Speed Skills	6 credits
03937	Speed Keying	5 credits
03938	Word Processing – English	6 credits
04606	Prosesu Geiriau	6 credits

Level 2 ITQ units

	Email	4 credits
	Presentation Software	6 credits
	Word Processing Software	6 credits

Level 3 ITQ units

	Email	6 credits
	Word Processing Software	8 credits

Group 3: optional units

Entry Level Text Processing units

06965	Speed Keying	2 credits

Level 1 Text Processing units

06967	Audio-Transcription	4 credits
06968	Business Presentations	4 credits

06969	Computer Keyboard Skills	3 credits
06970	Legal Text Processing	4 credits
06971	Mailmerge	4 credits
06972	Shorthand Speed Skills	4 credits
06973	Speed Keying	4 credits
06974	Word Processing – English	4 credits
03946	Prosesu Geiriau	4 credits

Level 1 ITQ units

	Email	2 credits
	Presentation Software	4 credits
	Word Processing Software	4 credits

Unit contents

The following syllabuses give details of the unit contents for Text Processing, Word Processing and Audio-Transcription at Level 2.

The first section of each syllabus covers the following aspects.

- **Learning outcomes:** listed in the first column of the table, these describe the tasks that you will be able to carry out once you have acquired the necessary skills to complete the exam at this level.
- **Assessment criteria:** described in the second column of the table, they show the way in which your skills will be assessed in the exam.
- **Knowledge, understanding and skills:** detailed in the third column of the table, they describe the information you need to enable you to complete the exam.

The second section of each document covers the following:

- Unit aim
- Assessment
- Administration guidance
- Guidance on assessment and evidence requirements.

The third section of each document covers the following:

- **Marking criteria:** described in the first column of the table, they show the ways in which your work will be assessed.
- **Tutor notes:** listed in the second column of the table, these give further details about how an exam is marked. Although drafted for tutors, this information will give you invaluable help when you are working towards the exam.

These units are updated periodically. The most up-to-date versions of these syllabuses can be accessed on the Text Processing page of the OCR website: www.ocr.org.uk

TEXT PROCESSING (BUSINESS PROFESSIONAL)

Text Production

06975

Level:	2
Credits:	5
Learning Time:	50 hours

Learning Outcomes	Assessment Criteria	Knowledge, understanding and skills
1 Use a word processor or a typewriter efficiently	1.1 Use the different functions of a word processor or different parts of a typewriter	• Set top and left margins of at least 13 mm • Alter linespacing (single/double) as instructed • Emphasise text as instructed • Underline text as instructed
2 Enter and format text from handwritten and typewritten drafts	2.1 Produce text accurately and efficiently from manuscript and from typewritten drafts	• Plan and organise work within deadlines • Read and transcribe variable quality manuscript • Plan layout of work in a variety of formats • Accurately key in text from handwritten and typewritten drafts • Interpret written instructions • Check accuracy of amendments and that all instructions have been carried out correctly • Use English and mother-tongue dictionaries, calendars • Proofread and correct errors, using appropriate correction techniques, to ensure work is 100% accurate • Use consistent style and format of presentation with at least one clear linespace before and after separate items within a document • Use appropriate stationery, ie plain A4 paper

	2.2 Amend text as instructed	Amend text as shown in draft: • deletion with replacement words • deletion without replacement words • Follow correction signs:

new paragraph ⌈ or //

run on ⌐⌐

insertion with word(s) above ⋏ or balloon with arrow eg

transpose horizontally ∽ or balloon with arrow eg

transpose vertically

stet _ _ _ _ _ _ with (✓) in margin

} no marginal instructions

	2.3 Expand abbreviations, ensuring correct spellings	Expand abbreviations shown in the list below:

a/c(s)	account(s)	mtg(s)	meeting
approx	approximate(ly)	necy	necessary
asap	as soon as possible	opp(s)	opportunity(ies)
cat(s)	catalogue(s)	org(s)	organisation(s)
co(s)	company(ies)	poss	possible
doc(s)	document(s)	ref(d)	refer(red)
dr	dear	ref(s)	reference(s)
emp	employment	sec(s)	secretary(ies)
gntee(s)	guarantee(s)	sig(s)	signature(s)
immed	immediate(ly)	tel	telephone
info	information	temp	temporary
misc	miscellaneous	yr(s)	year(s)
mfr(s)	manufacturer(s)	yr(s)	your(s)

days of the week (eg Thur, Fri)
months of the year (eg Jan, Feb)
words in addresses (eg Rd, St, Ave, Dr, Sq, Cres, Pl, Pk)
complimentary close (eg ffly, sncly)

	2.4 Check and correct material containing typographical errors, errors of agreement, punctuation and spelling errors	Correct errors in the draft which will be indicated by circling the words: • errors of agreement including those of subject/verb and quantity/noun • apostrophe errors including misplaced and superfluous apostrophes

		Locate and correct errors in the draft which will not be indicated: • typographical errors including words containing extra, omitted and transposed letters and extraneous symbols • punctuation errors including omitted full stop and omitted initial capital at the start of a sentence • spelling errors in words given below including their derivations where marked * (eg plurals, prefixes (such as un-, in-, dis-, ir-) and suffixes (such as -ed, -ing, -ment, -tion, -ly, -able, -ible, -ence, -ial) access* discuss* accommodate* expense* achieve* experience* acknowledge* financial* advertise* foreign although govern* apparent* convenient* appreciate* receipt* believe* receive* business* recommend* client* responsible* colleague* separate* committee* sufficient* correspond* supplementary definite* temporary* develop* through
3 Produce three business documents	3.1 Key in and print a business letter from handwritten draft on OCR supplied letterhead	• Use conventional and consistent layout and style of a business letter • Insert today's date on letter • Use OCR supplied letterhead template • *Our ref* details are keyed in as shown in draft, including capitalisation • Insert a special mark eg URGENT, CONFIDENTIAL as indicated on the draft • Postdate as instructed • Indicate enclosures, if implied in the draft, using an acceptable convention • Underline words as indicated on the draft

	3.2 Key in and print a memo/press release/file note from handwritten draft on OCR supplied template	• Use conventional and consistent layout and style of a variety of business documents • Insert today's date against date heading • Must be produced on OCR supplied memo/press release/file note template • Indicate enclosures, if implied in the draft, using an acceptable convention
	3.3 Key in and print a report/article from handwritten and typewritten draft on plain A4 paper	• Use conventional and consistent layout and style of a report/article • Insert a page number on continuation sheets • Use single/double linespacing as instructed • Emphasise text, as instructed
	3.4 Key in and incorporate information from a separate sheet supplied as a distraction	• Deal with a distraction in the form of additional text to be included in the report/article

Unit aim

This unit aims to equip candidates with the ability to produce, from handwritten and typewritten draft material, a range of business documents to a standard that meets the business document production requirements of employment.

Assessment

Assessment will consist of producing three business documents totalling 750 words and will take the form of a 1 hour 15 minute test set and marked by OCR.

Results will be graded Distinction, Pass or Fail.

To achieve a Distinction, candidates must produce the documents with no more than 4 faults within the time allowed (1 hour 15 minutes).

To achieve a Pass, candidates must produce the documents with no more than 11 faults within the time allowed (1 hour 15 minutes).

The grade achieved will be stated on the certificate.

Administration guidance

- Either a word processor or a typewriter may be used to complete the exam.

- Stationery: A4 plain paper. Pre-printed templates will be required for those candidates using a typewriter.

- Printing: candidates **must** carry out their own printing.

- For further information regarding administration for this qualification, please refer to the OCR document '*Administrative Guide for Vocational Qualifications*' (A850).

Guidance on assessment and evidence requirements

Candidates must produce three business documents to a standard acceptable in the workplace and outcomes must be within the permitted error tolerance.

Penalties are given for errors and the same fault appearing more than once will incur a penalty each time. One fault only will be given to any one word* irrespective of the number of errors that may appear in that word. For example, "miscellaneous" keyed in as "miss-selanious" will be penalised 1 fault, even though several faults have been incurred in the word.

* A word is defined as any normally recognisable word including a hyphenated word and associated punctuation and spacing. Other items that are treated as a word are:

- postcode
- initials and courtesy titles
- simple or complex numbers including money, times and telephone numbers
- simple or compound measurements

You should refer to the '*OCR Administrative Guide to Vocational Qualifications (A850)*' for Notes on Preventing Computer-Assisted Malpractice.

Errors will be divided into 4 categories:

Marking Criteria	Tutor Notes
Section 1 Faults - keying in errors **One fault will be given for each word* which:**	
1.1 contains a character which is incorrect (including upper case character within a word), or is illegible for any reason	• A penalty will be incurred for any word that contains a character that is incorrect or that includes an upper case character within a word, eg *LaBel* • Candidates may use English and mother tongue dictionaries and spellcheckers where available
1.2 has omitted or additional characters or spaces (including omissions caused by faulty use of correction materials/techniques, eg hole in paper)	• A space inserted between a word and its associated punctuation, eg *word :* or *word ?* will incur 1 fault per instance • Incorrect or omitted paired punctuation eg brackets, single quotes will incur 1 fault per 'pair', eg (Progress Group), ' Progress Group '
1.3 contains handwritten character(s)	
1.4 has no space following it	

1.5 has more than 2 character spaces following it, except where appropriate, eg before postcode, after punctuation	In continuous text, 1 fault per instance will be incurred for: • more than 3 spaces appearing after a full stop, question mark, exclamation mark or colon • more than 2 spaces appearing after a comma, semi-colon, closing bracket, dash, apostrophe (at the end of a word) and closing single or double quotes • where a short line appears, this will be penalised if the first word following could have fitted at the end of the short line with at least 18 mm ($^3/_4$") to spare (measuring the short line against the longest line in the document)
1.6 contains overtyping, including overtyping of pre-printed material (per entry regardless of the number of words involved) eg text cutting through letterhead template	
1.7 does not contain initial capitals: - as presented in the draft - for the first letter of a sentence	• Candidates should key in text as presented in the draft. One fault per instance will be incurred for each initial capital drafted that has been keyed in as a lower case character • Failure to insert a capital letter following a penalty for an omitted full stop will not be penalised. Likewise, inserting a capital letter following a penalty for an incorrect full stop will not be penalised
Section 2 Faults - omissions and additions **One fault will be given for:**	
2.1 each word which is the wrong word and a word that has been omitted or added or not removed as instructed (eg a word which is crossed out in the draft)	• *Our ref* and reference details must be keyed as shown in draft, including capitalisation. Treat the whole reference as one unit for marking purposes. Errors in references incur one fault maximum per document • Candidates will incur a fault if they set up their own reference, or omit the reference, or add their own initials to the reference • In the letter the reference, date, special mark and name and address may be presented in any order but must appear above the salutation and must be keyed in as draft, including capitalisation • Any style of date is acceptable, with the exception of the American numeric format, eg *12/25/2009* as Christmas Day • Dates should appear below the letterhead and above the salutation of the letter and should have a clear linespace above/below • Dates will not be acceptable in the header/footer details alone • One fault will be incurred for each instance of a missing, incomplete or incorrect date to be inserted on correspondence as instructed on the front cover of the question paper

	• All errors in other dates are penalised per element
	• Where postdating is required, 1 fault maximum will be incurred for any errors or omissions
	• Omitted or additional text resulting from an attempt at vertical or horizontal transposition will be penalised 1 fault per word
	• If a date appears in a document that does not require dating, this will be penalised 1 fault maximum unless the date appears as part of the personal details
	Abbreviations
	Abbreviations in handwritten draft should be expanded correctly; failure to do so is penalised 1 fault per word
	NB: commonly used abbreviations must be retained, for example etc, eg, ie, NB, PS, plc, Ltd and & in company names
2.2 not applicable to this unit	
2.3 omission of implied or explicit instructions (regardless of the number of words involved) for failure to: - insert a special mark - indicate an enclosure - underline text - insert page numbers on continuation sheets	• Errors or omissions in a special mark will incur 1 fault maximum • Where enclosures are implied any appropriate method of indicating them may be used, eg *Enc Att Encs Atts*. Indications must differentiate between single and multiple enclosures • The indication of an enclosure must appear below the signatory details in the letter • Failure to underline words as shown in the draft or underline which is too short or too long incurs 1 fault (this is not treated as presentation which relates to the underlining of <u>headings</u> – see 4J below) • Page number on page 1 of a multi-page document is acceptable but page numbers on a single-page document will incur a penalty • Page numbers may appear in any position and may be any style but must appear once only on each page of a document • Errors and omissions related to page numbers are limited to 1 fault maximum per exam paper
Section 3 Faults - transpositions and misplacements **One fault will be given for each instance of:**	
3.1 items not transposed (horizontally or vertically) in accordance with a correction sign	• Failure to transpose items horizontally or vertically will be penalised 1 fault maximum per correction sign • Interim text (eg a paragraph or heading between the text to be transposed) which is misplaced as a direct result of the attempt to transpose will incur 1 fault maximum

3.2 words that are misplaced within text, where there is no instruction	• Words inserted in the wrong order or place in the absence of an instruction eg misplaced within text or as foot or marginal note, regardless of the amount of material involved (in addition to any faults that may be incurred above) • In a memo, transposition of entries against "To, From" headings incurs 1 fault per misplaced item
3.3 failure to paragraph as per draft or as specified by a correction sign, eg new paragraph or run on	

Section 4 Faults – presentation
No more than one fault per paper for each of the following items:

4A left and/or top margins of less than 13 mm, or ragged left margin	This includes: • ragged left margin, eg additional character spacing at the beginning of a line or paragraph • main and subheadings not keyed in at the left margin, as presented in draft – unless otherwise instructed (eg centring)
4B no clear linespace before and after separate items within a document	• Failure to leave a clear linespace before and after separate items within a document, eg before/after headings, between paragraphs • Failure to leave a clear linespace below a letter heading NB: Where letterhead template is centred or right aligned there is no requirement for a clear linespace below the letterhead. Where the letterhead template is left aligned, a clear linespace must be left
4C failure to use linespacing as instructed	This includes: • failure to change linespacing as instructed
4D failure to emphasise text as instructed	This includes: • emphasis extending beyond the required portion • additional emphasis of text where not requested (except for headings – see 4J below) Emphasis may be any method such as bold, italics, underlining, capitals, centring, change of font/size
4E not applicable to this unit	
4F not applicable to this unit	
4G work which is creased, torn or dirty (including conspicuous corrections)	• Invigilators should report any machine problems resulting in marks on paper • Invigilators should also report any problems with printers, so as not to disadvantage candidates
4H incorrect stationery used (ie OCR supplied templates, A4 plain paper, portrait/landscape)	• Failure to use OCR supplied letterhead, memo, press release and file note templates (tutors may print these for use with typewriters) • Failure to produce continuation sheets on plain paper • Page 1 of a report may be produced on plain or headed paper • Templates must not be altered in any way

4I inconsistent spacing between and within similar items within a document	• Inconsistent spacing (including linespacing) between and within similar items is only penalised if a comparison with a similar item can be made within the same document • Inconsistent linespacing above and below an item, for example, an inset portion, will not be penalised as there is no further instance of insetting within the same document for comparison

4J use of initial capitals where not presented in draft, or:
  - closed capitals used where not presented in draft
  - failure to use closed capitals as presented in draft
  - failure to key in headings with initial capitals and underlined as presented in draft
	This includes:
	• use of initial capitals where initial capitals were not presented in draft, eg *Sincerely* in complimentary close
	• closed capitals used where not presented in draft, eg *White* keyed in as *WHITE*
	  failure to use closed capitals as presented in draft, eg *DISEASES* keyed in as *Diseases*
	• failure to underline headings, including subheadings, as presented in the draft, eg "<u>Miscellaneous Household Items</u>" keyed in as "Miscellaneous Household Items"
	• capitalisation faults in postcodes
	• Candidates should key in data exactly as shown in the draft (except for circled words with errors of agreement and apostrophe errors and typographical, punctuation and spelling errors which will not be indicated) but additional emboldening, italicising or underlining of headings will not be penalised

4K inconsistent use of alternative spellings within a document	• Alternative spellings that may be found in an English dictionary will be accepted but a penalty will be incurred if that alternative spelling is used inconsistently, eg *organize* but *organisation* within the same document

4L inconsistent display of dates, measurements, weights, times, money, figures, dashes/hyphens	• Dates must be of consistent style throughout a document. For example, if full style is used such as *12 January 2009*, this style should be used for all subsequent dates within the same document. (Please also refer to Section 2.1 Notes above)
	• Measurements and weights must be used consistently. For example, *5cm* or *5 cm*; *16kg* or *16 kg*
	• Times should be keyed in as shown in the draft. Candidates should not change times from 12-hour clock to 24-hour clock or vice versa, unless instructed to do so
	• Money: there must be no character space between £ and the amount, eg *£60*
	• The display of figures should be an "acceptable system", eg
	  - all figures including "1"
	  - all words (but use of words such as *twenty-five* or *twenty five* must be consistent)
	  - *one* as a word, all others as figures

	- *one* to *nine* or *ten* as words and then *10* or *11* upwards as figures - *one* to *twenty* as words and then *21* upwards as figures • Where dashes or hyphens are used to represent the word "to" (eg *15-22* or *15 – 22*) these must be used consistently throughout a document
4M inconsistent use of open or full punctuation within a document	This includes: • a full stop appearing in any abbreviation such as enc, cc, eg, am, when open punctuation has been used • a missing full stop in any abbreviation such as enc., c.c., e.g., a.m., where full punctuation has been used
4N insertion of an additional comma which alters the meaning of a sentence	• Candidates should key in punctuation as presented in the draft. However, the insertion of an additional comma will only be penalised if this alters the meaning of the sentence

TEXT PROCESSING (BUSINESS PROFESSIONAL)

Word Processing
06999

Level:	2
Credits:	5
Learning Time:	50 hours

Learning Outcomes	Assessment Criteria	Knowledge, understanding and skills
1 Use a word processor efficiently	1.1 Use the different functions of a word processor	• Change left and top margins • Change linespacing • Use spellchecker • Use correct pagination • Number pages as specified • Insert a header or a footer in specified position • Search and Replace • Inset text • Change font and size • Centre text • Underline text • Set up a table with sub divided columns • Set up a column aligning decimal points • Merge cells • Use full justification • Move and copy text • Insert a picture and resize the width • Sort data alphabetically, numerically or chronologically • Recall pre-stored autotext phrases • Use word count facility • Print using portrait and landscape

Learning Outcomes	Assessment Criteria	Knowledge, understanding and skills
2 Input text from handwritten and typewritten drafts	2.1 Produce text accurately and efficiently from handwritten and from typewritten drafts and carry out own printing	• Plan and organise work within deadlines • Plan layout of work in a variety of formats • Interpret written instructions • Use consistent style and format of presentation with at least one clear linespace before and after separate items within a document • Read and transcribe variable quality manuscript • Accurately key in text from handwritten and typewritten drafts • Use English and mother-tongue dictionaries • Check accuracy of amendments and that all instructions have been carried out correctly • Use spellcheckers • Proofread and correct errors, to ensure work is 100% accurate • Use plain A4 paper • Print single and multi-page copies

Learning Outcomes	Assessment Criteria	Knowledge, understanding and skills

3 Produce four business documents	3.1 Retrieve an article/information sheet/report, amend as instructed and print one copy	• Correctly retrieve text from pre-stored document
		• Use conventional layout and style of an article/information sheet/report
		• Key in text
		• Adjust left and top margins
		• Use full justification
		• Move text
		• Copy text
		• Insert page breaks as specified
		• Insert a header or footer
		• Number pages 2 and 3
		• Search and replace
		• Amend text as instructed:
		  – deletion with replacement words
		  – deletion without replacement words
		• Follow correction signs
		
		New paragraph $\lceil$ or $/\!/$
		Run on $\frown$
		Insertion with word(s) above $\wedge$ or balloon with arrow
		Transpose horizontally or balloon with arrow eg
		
		Close up
		Stet – – – – – – with ✓ in margin
		
		• Change linespacing of document to double linespacing, as instructed
		• Inset a section of text from the left
		• Print multi-page document on plain A4 paper

Learning Outcomes	Assessment Criteria	Knowledge, understanding and skills

	3.2 Recall a notice/poster/ advertisement for display, amend as instructed and print one copy	• Correctly retrieve text from pre-stored file
		• Ensure left and top margins are at least 13 mm
		• Centre one or more lines of text
		• Underline words which will be included in handwritten text in the draft
		• Change font size of a section of text
		• Insert a picture, resize width and wrap text to left/right as instructed
		• Sort a recalled list
		• Amend text as instructed:
		  – deletion without replacement words
		• Follow correction signs
		  – insertion: ⋏
		  – transpose consecutive items vertically
		  – leave a space /
		• Use software facilities to perform a word count
		• Print one copy on a single sheet of A4 landscape

	3.3 Recall a document and key in a table and continuous text from handwritten draft and print one copy	• Correctly retrieve text in Arial 11 from pre-stored file • Ensure left and top margins are at least 13 mm • Key in document in Arial 11 from handwritten draft • Allocate vertical space • Key in a main heading, section headings and column headings (one sub-divided) in all capitals • Key in four columns and two sections of data containing text and numbers • Ensure text and data in columns and column headings are left aligned consistently

Learning Outcomes	Assessment Criteria	Knowledge, understanding and skills
		• Ensure decimal points are aligned consistently and that the longest figure is left aligned with the column heading • Display lines of text in the sections of the table as copy • Sort columns into a specified order • Carry out one aspect of modification, eg change the sequence of columns or change the order of sections • Print one copy of the document on a single sheet of A4 portrait
	3.4 Key in a letter on a pre-stored letterhead template from handwritten draft. Retrieve autotext phrases and print and route copies as instructed	• Correctly retrieve pre-stored letterhead • Key in letter from handwritten draft using letterhead template provided by OCR • Use conventional layout and style of a business letter • Insert today's date • Key in *Our ref* details including capitalisation • Produce extra copies and indicate routing of copies. Destination details may be included on the top copy but must be present on the extra copies • Ensure left and top margins are at least 13 mm • Insert two autotext phrases • Ensure consistent display of bullet points in recalled and keyed in text • Use specified font and size ensuring consistency • Use ragged/justified margins as requested • Number second page

Learning Outcomes	Assessment Criteria	Knowledge, understanding and skills
		• Print document and 2 extra copies with first page on recalled letterhead template

Unit aim

This unit aims to equip candidates with the ability to produce, from handwritten and recalled text using a word processor, a variety of business documents to a standard that meets the requirements of employment.

Assessment

Assessment will consist of producing four business documents totalling 1020 +/– 20 words (totalling 500 words to be input and 520 +/– 20 words to be recalled) in the time allowed and will take the form of a 1 hour 45 minute test set and marked by OCR.

Results will be graded Distinction, Pass or Fail.

To achieve a Distinction, candidates must produce the documents with no more than 4 faults within the time allowed (1 hour 45 minutes).

To achieve a Pass, candidates must produce the documents with no more than 11 faults within the time allowed (1 hour 45 minutes).

The grade achieved will be stated on the certificate.

Administration guidance

•   Word processing equipment **must** be used to complete the exam

•   Centres must ensure that the recall material for this examination is available for candidates. This includes a letterhead template. The autotext phrases are stored within the letterhead template. This recall material will be available on CD-ROM provided by OCR or can be downloaded from Interchange, OCR's secure website

•   Centres **must not** re-key or amend the pre-stored documents, or letterhead. Centres must check that the autotext phrases work on their system and if necessary key in the autotext phrases in the letterhead template file.

•   Stationery: A4 plain paper will be required

•   Printing: Candidates **must** carry out their own printing

•   For further information regarding administration for this qualification, please refer to the OCR document '*Administrative Guide for Vocational Qualifications*' *(A850).*

Guidance on assessment and evidence requirements

Candidates must produce four business documents to a standard acceptable in the workplace and outcomes must be within the permitted error tolerance.

Penalties are given for errors and the same fault appearing more than once will incur a penalty each time. One fault only will be given to any one word* irrespective of the number of errors that may appear in that word. For example, "miscellaneous" keyed in as "miss-selanious" will be penalised 1 fault, even though several faults have been incurred in the word.

* A word is defined as any normally recognisable word including a hyphenated word and associated punctuation and spacing. Other items that are treated as a word are:

- postcode
- initials and courtesy titles
- simple or complex numbers including money, times and telephone numbers
- simple or compound measurements

You should refer to the 'OCR Administrative Guide to Vocational Qualifications (A850)' for Notes on Preventing Computer-Assisted Malpractice.

Errors will be divided into 4 categories:

Marking Criteria	Tutor Notes
Section 1 Faults - keying in errors **One fault will be given for each word* which:**	
1.1 contains a character which is incorrect (including upper case character within a word), or is illegible for any reason	• A penalty will be incurred for any word that contains a character that is incorrect or that includes an upper case character within a word, eg *LaBel* • Candidates may use English and mother tongue dictionaries and spellcheckers where available
1.2 has omitted or additional characters or spaces (including omissions caused by faulty use of correction materials/techniques)	• A space inserted between a word and its associated punctuation, eg *word :* or *word ?* will incur 1 fault per instance • Incorrect or omitted paired punctuation eg brackets, single quotes will incur 1 fault per pair eg (Progress Group), ' Progress Group '
1.3 contains handwritten character(s)	
1.4 has no space following it	
1.5 has more than 2 character spaces following it, except where appropriate, eg before postcode, after punctuation	In continuous text, 1 fault per instance will be incurred for: • More than 3 spaces appearing after a full stop, question mark, exclamation mark or colon • More than 2 spaces appearing after a comma, semi-colon, closing bracket, dash, apostrophe (at the end of a word) and closing single or double quotes • Where a short line appears, this will be penalised if the first word following could have fitted at the end of the short line with at least 18 mm ($3/4''$) to spare (measuring the short line against the longest line in the document))
1.6 contains overtyping, including overtyping of pre-printed material (per entry regardless of the number of words involved) eg text cutting through letterhead template	

Marking Criteria	Tutor Notes
1.7 does not contain initial capitals as presented in the draft, including the first letter of a sentence	• Candidates should key in text as presented in the draft. One fault per instance will be incurred for each initial capital drafted that has been keyed in as a lower case character • Failure to insert a capital letter following a penalty for an omitted full stop will not be penalised Likewise inserting a capital letter following a penalty for an incorrect full stop will not be penalised

Marking Criteria	Tutor Notes
Section 2 Faults – omissions and additions **One fault will be given for:**	
2.1 each word which is the wrong word and a word that has been omitted or added or not removed as instructed (eg a word which is crossed out in the draft)	• Failure to delete recalled text and insert replacement words will incur 1 fault per wrong word or for each word that has been omitted • The unspecified deletion and/or duplication of recalled text will incur 1 fault per word, unless it can be attributed to a vertical or horizontal transposition, deletion without replacement (NB see 2.2 below), move or copy • One fault will be incurred for each instance of a missing, incomplete or incorrect date to be inserted on correspondence as instructed on the front cover of the question paper • All errors in other dates are penalised per element • The date should appear below the letterhead and above the salutation of the letter and should have a clear linespace above/below • Dates will not be acceptable in the header/footer details alone • Any style of date is acceptable, with the exception of the American numerical format, eg *12/25/2009* as Christmas Day • If a date appears in a document that does not require dating, this will be penalised 1 fault maximum unless the date appears as part of the personal details or above the first line of the document or below the last line of the document • Our reference details must be keyed in as shown in the draft, including capitalisation. Treat the whole reference as one unit for marking purposes. Errors in references incur one fault maximum per document. • Candidates will incur one fault if they set up their own reference, or omit the reference or add their own initials to the reference
2.2 each instance of failure to: 　– delete recalled text as instructed 　– produce an extra copy	• Failure to delete recalled text as shown in the draft will incur 1 fault maximum, irrespective of the number of words involved (this relates to a deletion where there are no replacement words written above the words crossed through) • Penalise 1 fault for each copy not produced
2.3 omission of implied or explicit instructions (regardless of the number of words involved) for failure to 　– recall correct autotext phrases 　– ensure consistent use of font style/size throughout a document	• Failure to recall each correct autotext phrase or for each phrase not recalled in full 1 fault per phrase • Duplication of any part of a phrase penalise 1 fault maximum per phrase

Marking Criteria	Tutor Notes
– change the font style/size as instructed – display bullet points consistently – insert a header/footer – number pages as specified – carry out an aspect of modification as instructed – insert and resize a picture as instructed – wrap text left/right of picture – underline text – indicate additional destination on all copies – indicate routing on appropriate extra copy – insert the total word count – column headings in table as copy – merge cells over sub-divided columns	• Changes made to the font style/size in a document where there is no instruction to do so will incur 1 fault maximum per exam paper • Failure to use a specified font style/size as instructed will incur 1 fault maximum per document • Failure to display bullet points consistently within a document 1 fault maximum (eg variable style, spacing) • Failure to insert a header/footer as instructed in the specified position incurs 1 fault maximum (including keying errors). Capitalisation faults may be penalised under 4J (see below) in addition. Headers/footers may appear within the top/bottom margin allowance • Any font style and size may be used in the header/footer area • Unrequested headers/footers eg DRAFT COPY incur 1 fault maximum • Candidates will not be penalised for putting their personal details in the header/footer • Failure to insert page numbers as instructed incurs 1 fault maximum • Insertion of page numbers on single-page documents incurs 1 fault maximum • Failure to insert page numbers on continuation sheets, 1 fault maximum is incurred • Page numbers may appear in any position and may be any style but must appear once only on each page of a document • Errors and omissions related to page numbers are limited to 1 fault maximum per exam paper • Failure to carry out an aspect of modification, eg change the sequence of columns in a table or change the sequence of sections in a table, not replacing the specified word in the search and replace, not inserting specified page breaks will incur 1 fault maximum irrespective of the number of words for failure to carry out each modification • The word used in search and replace will be keyed in consistently, eg SHARE, Share, share • Failure to insert the correct picture and/or re-size as instructed will incur 3 faults maximum – 1 each for failure to insert, size and wrap picture as instructed. Measurements of the picture must be accurate within a 1 mm tolerance

Marking Criteria	Tutor Notes
	• Failure to underline a word or words within the text or underlining is too short or too long as shown in the draft incurs 1 fault (this is not treated as presentation which relates to the underlining of <u>headings</u> – see 4J below.)
	• Failure to insert the destination details on the extra copies. These may include the words 'file' or 'files'
	• Errors, omissions etc relating to extra copies, destination details and routing will be penalised as 2 faults maximum
	• The destination details must include the word "copy", "cc" or similar – if not, 1 fault will be incurred
	• If addressee's name is included in destination details, 1 fault maximum will be incurred
	• Any method of indication of routing will be accepted
	• The word count will be evidenced by candidates keying in the figure below the final line of text
	• An incorrect word count will incur 1 fault maximum, eg candidates perform the word count at the wrong time
	• An incorrect word count resulting from errors in the text will not be penalised
	• Failure to remove gridlines will incur 1 fault
	• Adjust table column widths to ensure text is displayed on one line – wrapping text will incur 1 fault maximum
	• Heading over two sub-divided columns must span over the second sub-column

Marking Criteria	Tutor Notes
Section 3 Faults - transpositions and misplacements	
One fault will be given for each instance of:	
3.1 items not transposed (horizontally or vertically) in accordance with a correction sign	• Failure to transpose items in recalled text (horizontally or vertically) in accordance with an amendment sign will incur 1 fault per correction sign • Words that have been omitted as a direct result of incorrect horizontal or vertical transposition of recalled text incurs 1 fault maximum • Where vertically transposed text includes an amendment to text (eg deletion with replacement words) or a correction sign for insertion of words (eg caret sign, balloon or 'stet'), 1 fault per word for wrong/omitted words will be incurred under 2.1, in addition to the penalty under 3.1
3.2 words that are misplaced within text, where there is no instruction	
3.3 failure to paragraph as per draft or as specified by a correction sign, eg new paragraph or run on	
3.4 a list of items not sorted as instructed	• Failure to sort a list as instructed will incur 1 fault maximum. Any omitted, additional or incorrect words will be penalised 1 fault per word under 2.1 • Failure to ensure that corresponding details are correctly rearranged in the table sort will incur 1 fault maximum
3.5 failure to copy text as instructed	1 fault maximum will be incurred for: • failure to copy text within a document as instructed • copying the wrong text • moving the text rather than copying text
3.6 failure to move text as instructed	1 fault maximum will be incurred for: • failure to move text as instructed • moving the wrong text • copying text rather than moving text • all or part of the text moved is duplicated or missing
Section 4 Faults – presentation	
No more than one fault per paper for each of the following items:	
4A left and top margins of less than 13 mm or ragged left margin	• Ragged left margin, eg additional character spacing at the beginning of a line or paragraph • Main and subheadings not keyed in at the left margin, as presented in draft – unless otherwise instructed (eg centring) or recalled • section headings in table must appear as draft • the table may be inset from left margin but if table extends into the left margin resulting in an irregular left margin with text above/below table a fault will be incurred

Marking Criteria	Tutor Notes
4B no clear linespace before and after separate items within a document	• Failure to leave a clear linespace before and after separate items within a document, eg before/after headings, between paragraphs • Where letterhead template is centred or right aligned there is no requirement for a clear linespace below the letterhead. Where letterhead template is left aligned a clear linespace must be left.
4C failure to use linespacing as instructed	• Failure to change linespacing as instructed
4D failure to emphasise text as instructed	• Additional emphasis of text where not requested (except for headings – see 4J below) • Failure to clearly change the font or size of some text as instructed will incur a penalty. Note that if the changes are not clear, eg using similar sans serif fonts or changing the font size by one point, a penalty will be incurred
4E allocation of space not as instructed	• Failure to leave the minimum vertical space specified will incur a penalty
4F failure to centre text as instructed	• Failure to centre text as instructed to within 13 mm over the typing line
4G work which is creased, torn or dirty (including conspicuous corrections)	• Invigilators must notify OCR of any machine faults resulting in marks on the paper • Invigilators should also report any problems with printers, so as not to disadvantage candidates
4H incorrect stationery used (eg letterhead, A4 plain paper, portrait/landscape)	• Failure to use OCR letterhead templates • Failure to use landscape where requested • Failure to produce continuation sheets on plain paper • Complimentary close/routing details split over 2 pages will incur 1 fault maximum • Page 1 of a report may be produced on plain or headed paper • Templates must not be altered in any way
4I inconsistent spacing between and within similar items within a document	• Inconsistent spacing (including linespacing) between and within similar items is only penalised if a comparison with a similar item can be made within the same document • Inconsistent linespacing above and below an item, for example an inset portion, will not be penalised as there is no further instance of insetting within the same document for comparison

4J use of initial capitals where not presented in draft, or
  – closed capitals used where not presented in draft,
  – failure to use closed capitals as presented in draft,
  – failure to key in headings with initial capitals and underlined as presented in draft
	This includes:
	• Use of initial capitals where initial capitals were not presented in draft, eg *Sincerely* in complimentary close
	• Closed capitals used where not presented in draft, eg *White* keyed in as *WHITE*
	• Failure to use closed capitals as presented in draft, eg *DISEASES* keyed in as *Diseases*
	• Failure to underline headings, including subheadings, as presented in the draft, eg "<u>Miscellaneous Household Items</u>" keyed in as "Miscellaneous Household Items"

Marking Criteria	Tutor Notes
	• Capitalisation faults in postcodes • Candidates should key in data exactly as shown in the draft but additional emboldening, italicising or underlining of headings will not be penalised.
4K inconsistent use of alternative spellings within a document	• Alternative spellings that may be found in an English dictionary will be accepted but a penalty will be incurred if that alternative spelling is used inconsistently, eg *organize* but *organisation* within the same document

4L inconsistent display of dates, measurements, weights, times, money, figures, dashes/hyphens, lines of ruling within a document	• Dates must be of consistent style throughout a document. For example, if full style is used such as *12 January 2009*, this style should be used for all subsequent dates within the same document. (Please also refer to Section 2.1 Notes above.)
	• Measurements and weights must be used consistently. For example, *5 cm* or *5cm*; *16 kg* or *16kg*
	• Times must be keyed in consistently within a document eg *10.30am* and *2.30 pm* within the same document would incur a penalty. Candidates must ensure that times that they key in are consistent with those that appear in recalled text within a document. Candidates must not change times from 12-hour clock to 24-hour clock or vice versa unless instructed to do so.'
	• Money: there must be no character space between £ and the amount, eg *£60*. In columns and tables accept spacing between £ and amount
	• Figures with multiple digits can be keyed in with or without a comma, eg 10,000 or 10000. Inconsistency will be penalised
	• The display of figures should be an "acceptable system", eg
	  – all figures including "1"
	  – all words (but use of words such as *twenty-five* or *twenty five* must be consistent)
	  – *one* as a word, all others as figures
	  – *one* to *nine* or *ten* as words and then *10* or *11* upwards as figures
	  – *one* to *twenty* as words and then *21* upwards as figures
	• Where dashes or hyphens are used to represent the word "to" (eg *15-22* or *15 – 22*) these must be used consistently throughout a document

4M inconsistent use of open or full punctuation within a document	• a full stop appearing in any abbreviation such as Enc, CC, eg, am, when open punctuation has been used • a missing full stop in any abbreviation such as Enc., C.C., e.g., a.m., where full punctuation has been used

Marking Criteria	Tutor Notes
4N insertion of an additional comma which alters the meaning of a sentence	• Candidates should key in punctuation as presented in the draft. However, the insertion of an additional comma will only be penalised if this alters the meaning of the sentence
4O not applicable to this unit	

4P
   – failure to align text and figures in columns to the left consistently
   – failure to align data in columns consistently with column headings	

4Q failure to align the decimal points in column of numbers	• Where sums of money require the alignment of decimal points in columns, the first figure of the longest amount in each column should be left-aligned with the column heading
4R not applicable to this unit	
4S failure to justify text or data as instructed	A penalty will be incurred: • where right margin justification requested but left margin is ragged • if justification is lost on last line of page • if justification used when a right ragged margin is requested
4T failure to adjust margins or line length as instructed	• Left and top margin must be adjusted as instructed, within a 3 mm tolerance • Adjusting other margins as well as or instead of the left or top margin will incur 1 fault
4U failure to inset from left margin as instructed	• The inset measurement must be exactly as instructed. If extra text has been incorrectly included within the insetting, a penalty will be incurred • Insetting the wrong section of text incurs 1 fault maximum

TEXT PROCESSING
(BUSINESS PROFESSIONAL)
Audio-Transcription
06976

Level:	2
Credits:	4
Learning Time:	40 hours

Learning outcomes	Assessment criteria	Knowledge, understanding and skills
1 Use audio equipment, word processor or a typewriter effectively	1.1 Use the different functions of a word processor or different parts of a typewriter in co-ordination with audio equipment	• Set top and left margins of at least 13 mm • Alter linespacing (single/double) as instructed • Emphasise text as instructed eg emboldening, underlining, capitals, etc • Interpreting dictated text, eg knowledge of English grammar and correct spelling, use a spellchecker, etc • Understanding of verbal instructions for punctuation eg full stop (.) comma (,) oblique (/) etc
2 Enter and format text from recorded material	2.1 Produce text accurately and efficiently from Information Sheet and recorded material	• Plan and organise work within deadlines • Plan layout of work in a variety of formats • Accurately key in text from recorded speech • Interpret audio instructions • Proofread and correct errors, using appropriate correction techniques, to ensure work is 100% accurate • Use consistent style and format of presentation with at least one clear linespace before and after separate items within a document

			• Use English and mother-tongue dictionaries • Use appropriate stationery, ie plain A4 paper • Check accuracy of amendments and that all instructions have been carried out correctly
3 Produce business documents	3.1	Key in and print a business letter on a pre-printed letterhead or by use of a template from recorded material	• Use conventional and consistent layout and style of a business letter • Use OCR supplied letterhead template • *Our ref* detail is keyed in as shown on the information sheet, including capitalisation • Insert today's date on letter • Insert a special mark, as dictated eg Private and Confidential, Urgent, etc • Insert a subject heading as dictated • Indicate enclosure(s), as implied in the verbal instruction, using an acceptable convention • Produce extra copies and indicate routing on each copy. Destination details may be included on the top copy but must be present on the extra copies
	3.2	Key in and print a memo, advertisement or notice from recorded material	• Use conventional and consistent layout and style of a variety of business documents • Insert reference detail as given on the information sheet where appropriate (ie the memo) • Insert today's date against date heading on memo • Memo must be produced on OCR template • Insert headings as dictated

		• Emphasise text, as instructed eg emboldening, underlining, capitals • Centre over the typing line • Produce numbered paragraphs or items as instructed
	3.3 Key in and print an article or report from recorded material	• Use conventional and consistent layout and style of a report or article • Insert a page number on continuation sheets, if used • Use single/double linespacing as instructed • Insert a subject heading as dictated • Key in a table as dictated • Change linespacing as instructed • Allocate vertical space as instructed • Include distraction element
	3.4 Amend word corrections as dictated	
	3.5 Insert a table within text	• Key in a table from recorded speech • Key in three or four columns of data containing text and numbers • Ensure data in columns and column headings are aligned consistently

Unit aim

This unit aims to equip candidates with the ability to produce a variety of routine business documents to a standard that meets the business document production requirements of employment from recorded speech and information provided on the information sheet.

Assessment

Assessment will consist of producing three business documents totalling 600 words and will take the form of a 1 hour 30 minute test set and marked by OCR.

In order to subject the candidates to distraction, extra details for Document 3 will be announced by the Invigilator approximately 15–30 minutes after the start of work.

Candidates will be required to work from recorded speech containing interpolations and corrections to produce 3 documents. The dictation will be given by means of a recording played on equipment over which the candidates have individual control.

Results will be graded Distinction, Pass or Fail.

To achieve a Distinction, candidates must produce the documents with no more than 3 faults within the time allowed (1 hour 30 minutes).

To achieve a Pass, candidates must produce the documents with no more than 9 faults within the time allowed (1 hour 30 minutes).

The grade achieved will be stated on the certificate.

Administration guidance

- Either a word processor or a typewriter may be used to complete the exam.

- Dictation for Audio-Transcription is recorded and supplied by OCR as mp3 and .wav files on CD-ROM and downloadable from OCR Interchange. The material must be copied onto equipment over which the candidates have individual control.

- Centres **must not** re-key or amend the pre-stored documents.

- Stationery: A4 plain paper. Pre-printed templates will be required for those candidates using a typewriter.

- Printing: Candidates **must** carry out their own printing. (Photocopying may be undertaken by an appointed person but routing must be undertaken by the candidate).

- Audio equipment to be supplied by the Centre.

- For further information regarding administration for this qualification, please refer to the OCR document 'Administrative Guide for Vocational Qualifications' (A850).

Guidance on assessment and evidence requirements

Candidates must produce three business documents to a standard acceptable in the workplace and outcomes must be within the permitted error tolerance.

Penalties are given for errors and the same fault appearing more than once will incur a penalty each time. One fault only will be given to any one word* irrespective of the number of errors that may appear in that word. For example "miscellaneous" keyed in as "miss-selanious" will be penalised 1 fault, even though several faults have been incurred in the word.

* A word is defined as any normally recognisable word including a hyphenated word and associated punctuation and spacing. Other items that are treated as a word are:

- postcode
- initials and courtesy titles
- simple or complex numbers including money, times and telephone numbers
- simple or compound measurements

Invigilators are given clear instructions to report any problems with printers, failure to do so can disadvantage their candidate(s).

You should refer to the 'OCR Administrative Guide to Vocational Qualifications (A850)' for Notes on Preventing Computer-Assisted Malpractice.

Errors will be divided into 4 categories:

Marking criteria	Tutor Notes
Section 1 Faults – keying in errors	
One fault will be given for each word* which:	
1.1 contains a character which is incorrect (including upper case character within a word), or is illegible for any reason	• A penalty will be incurred for any word that contains a character that is incorrect or that includes an upper case character within a word, eg *LaBel* • Candidates may use English and mother tongue dictionaries and spellcheckers where available
1.2 has omitted or additional characters or spaces (including omissions caused by faulty use of correction materials/techniques, eg hole in paper)	• A space inserted between a word and its associated punctuation, eg *word : or word ?* will incur 1 fault per instance • Incorrect or omitted paired punctuation, eg brackets, single quotes will incur 1 fault per 'pair', eg (Progress Group), ' Progress Group '
1.3 contains handwritten character(s)	
1.4 has no space following it	
1.5 has more than 2 character spaces following it, except where appropriate, eg before postcode, after punctuation	In continuous text, 1 fault per instance will be incurred for: • More than 3 spaces appearing after a full stop, question mark, exclamation mark or colon • More than 2 spaces appearing after a comma, semi-colon, closing bracket, dash, apostrophe (at the end of a word) and closing single or double quotes • Where a short line appears, this will be penalised if the first word following could have fitted at the end of the short line with at least 18 mm (^{3}/$_4$″) to spare (measuring the short line against the longest line in the document)
1.6 contains overtyping, including overtyping of pre-printed material (per entry regardless of the number of words involved) eg text cutting through letterhead template	
1.7 does not contain initial capitals: - as presented on the information sheet - for the first letter of a sentence	• Candidates should key in text as dictated. One fault per instance will be incurred for each initial capital presented on the information sheet that has been keyed in as a lower case character. • Initial capitals will not be dictated for proper nouns or at the beginning of sentences. One fault per instance will be incurred for each initial capital that has been keyed in as a lower case character for proper nouns or at the beginning of a sentence

	• Failure to insert a capital letter following a penalty for an omitted full stop will not be penalised. Likewise, inserting a capital letter following a penalty for an incorrect full stop will not be penalised
Section 2 Faults – omissions and additions	
One fault will be given for:	
2.1 each word which is the wrong word and a word that that has been omitted or added	• Any style of *Our ref* is acceptable, but candidates will incur a fault if they set up their own reference (not as dictated or on the information sheet), or omit the reference, or add their own initials to the reference • The reference, date, name and address may be presented in any order but must appear above the salutation and must be keyed in as given on the information sheet, including capitalisation • The subject heading must appear somewhere between the letterhead details and the first paragraph of the letter and must be keyed in as dictated • Any style of date is acceptable, with the exception of the American numerical format, eg *12/25/2009* as *Christmas Day* • Dates should appear below the letterhead and above the salutation of the letter and should have a clear linespace above/below • Dates will not be acceptable in the header/footer details alone • One fault will be incurred for each instance of a missing, incomplete or incorrect date to be inserted on correspondence as instructed on the front cover of the question paper • All errors in other dates are penalised per element unless otherwise specified • Where postdating is required, one fault maximum will be incurred for any errors or omissions • If a date appears in a document that does not require dating, this will be penalised 1 fault max unless the date appears as part of the personal details or above the first line of the document or below the last line of the document

2.2
   -   failure to indicate routing as dictated
   -   failure to produce extra copies
	• Two extra copies must be produced, either by photocopying, additional printouts or from typewriter memory
	
	• Failure to produce extra copies will be penalised 1 fault per copy missing

	• Errors relating to extra copies, such as errors, omissions in destination details, or incorrect or omitted routing are limited to 2 faults maximum
	• Copies may be produced on the OCR template or plain A4 paper, if using a typewriter
2.3 omission of implied or explicit instructions (regardless of the number of words involved) for failure to: - insert a subject heading - insert a special mark eg Private and Confidential, Urgent - indicate an enclosure - insert page numbers on continuation sheet - indicate additional destination on all copies - indicate routing on appropriate extra copy	• Errors or omission in a subject heading will incur 1 fault max • Errors or omissions in a special mark will incur 1 fault max • Where enclosures are implied, any method of indicating them may be used, eg *Enc, Att, Encs, Atts.* Indications must differentiate between single and multiple enclosures • The indication of an enclosure must appear between the signatory details and the footer • Page number on page 1 of a multi-page document is acceptable but page numbers on a single-page document will incur a penalty • Page numbers may appear in any position and may be any style but must appear once only on each page of a document • Errors and omissions related to page numbers are limited to 1 fault max per exam paper • If numbers in a numbered list are omitted, 1 fault maximum is incurred • The destination details must appear on all copies of the letter. These may include 'file' or 'files' • The destination details must include the word "copy" "cc" or similar – if not, 1 fault will be incurred • If addressee's name is included in destination details, 1 fault max will be incurred • Any method of indication of routing will be accepted, eg "tick", special mark or character, emphasis such as bold, underline or use of highlighter pen • Indicate special mark as instructed

Section 3 Faults – transpositions and misplacements	
One fault will be given for each instance of:	
3.1 not applicable to this unit	
3.2 words that are misplaced within text, where there is no instruction	This includes: • words inserted in the wrong order or place in the absence of an instruction eg misplaced within text or as foot or marginal note, regardless of the amount of material involved (in addition to any faults that may be incurred above)
	• each incorrect insertion of an entry against a pre-printed or template item
3.3 failure to paragraph as per verbal instruction	
Section 4 Faults – presentation	
No more than one fault per paper for each of the following items:	
4A left and/or top margins of less than 13 mm, or ragged left margin	This includes: • ragged left margin, eg additional character spacing at the beginning of a line or paragraph • main and sub-headings not keyed in at the left margin, in the absence of an alternative instruction
4B no clear linespace before and after separate items within a document	• Failure to leave a clear linespace before and after separate items within a document, eg before/after headings, between paragraphs • One-line numbered paragraphs are acceptable in any consistent linespacing, including no clear linespacing NB: Where letterhead template is centred or right aligned there is no requirement for a clear linespace below the letterhead. Where letterhead template is left aligned, a clear linespace must be left
4C failure to use linespacing as instructed	This includes: • failure to change linespacing as instructed • accept one clear linespace after heading before table text in single linespacing • accept one, two or three single linespaces before table text in double linespacing
4D failure to emphasise text as instructed	This includes: • emphasis extended beyond the required portion • additional emphasis of text where not requested (except for headings – see 4J below) Emphasis may be any method such as bold, italics or underlining

4E	allocation of space not as instructed	
4F	failure to centre text or data as instructed	• Failure to centre text or data as instructed to within 13 mm over the typing line
4G	work which is creased, torn or dirty (including conspicuous corrections)	• Errors on copies that did not appear on the top copy will be penalised under 4G • Invigilators should report any machine problems resulting in marks on paper • Invigilators should also report any problems with printers, so as not to disadvantage candidates
4H	incorrect stationery used (ie OCR supplied template, A4 plain paper)	• The first page of a report may be produced on plain or headed paper • failure to use OCR templates • Templates must not be altered in any way
4I	inconsistent spacing between and within similar items within a document	• Inconsistent spacing (including linespacing) between and within similar items is only penalised if a comparison with a similar item can be made within the same document
		• Inconsistent linespacing above and below an item, for example; an inset portion, will not be penalised as there is no further instance of insetting within the same document for comparison
4J	use of initial capitals where not presented on the information sheet or: - closed capitals used where not dictated - failure to use closed capitals as dictated - failure to key in headings with initial capitals and underline as dictated	This includes: • use of initial capitals where initial capitals were not dictated eg *Sincerely* in complimentary close • headings with initial capitals are acceptable as: Facilities in all Conference Rooms, or Facilities In All Conference Rooms • closed capitals where not dictated or presented on the information sheet eg *White* keyed in as *WHITE* • failure to use closed capitals as dictated eg *DISEASES* keyed in as *Diseases* • failure to underline headings, including subheadings, as dictated, eg "Miscellaneous Household Items" keyed in as "Miscellaneous Household Items" • capitalisation faults in postcodes • Candidates should key in data exactly as dictated and as given on the information sheet but additional emboldening, italicising or underlining of headings will not be penalised

4K	inconsistent use of alternative spellings within a document	•	Alternative spellings that may be found in an English dictionary will be accepted but a penalty will be incurred if that alternative spelling is used inconsistently, eg *organize* but *organisation* within the same document
4L	inconsistent display of dates, measurements, weights, times, money, figures, dashes/hyphens, lines of ruling within a document	•	Dates must be of consistent style throughout a document. For example, if full style is used such as *12 January 2009*, this style should be used for all subsequent dates within the same document. (Please also refer to Section (2.1) Notes above)
		•	Measurements and weights must be used consistently. For example, *5 cm* or *5cm*; *16 kg* or *16kg*
		•	Times should be keyed in as dictated. Candidates should not change times from 12-hour clock to 24-hour clock or vice versa, unless instructed to do so
		•	Money; there must be no character space between £ and the amount, eg *£60*. However, in columns and tables accept spacing between £ and amount
		•	- The display of figures should be an "acceptable system", eg - all figures including "1" - all words (but use of words such as twenty-five or twenty five must be consistent)one as a word, all others as figures - one to nine or ten as words and the 10 or 11 upwards as figures - one to twenty as words and then 21 upwards as figures
		•	Where dashes or hyphens are used to represent the word "to" (eg 15-22 or 15 – 22) these must be used consistently throughout a document
		•	Lines of ruling in a table – a candidate opting to use gridlines in a table will incur a penalty only if these result in empty cells
		•	Where lines of ruling have been inserted, a penalty under 4B will not be incurred for failure to leave a clear linespace below the column headings
		•	Any consistent style of numbered paragraphs/items is acceptable eg 1 1) 1. or (1)

4M	inconsistent use of open or full punctuation within a document	This includes: • A full stop appearing in any abbreviation such as enc, cc, eg, am when open punctuation has been used • A missing full stop in any abbreviation such as enc., c.c., e.g., a.m. where full punctuation has been used
4N	insertion of an additional comma which alters the meaning of a sentence	• Candidates should key in punctuation as dictated. However, the insertion of an additional comma will only be penalised if this alters the meaning of the sentence

4P	failure to align text and figures in columns to the left consistently
	   - failure to align figures in columns to the left, right or centre consistently
	   - failure to align data in columns consistently with column headings
		• Where sums of money require the alignment of decimal points in a column, the first figure should be left-aligned with the column heading

4Q	failure to align decimal points within a document	

KNOWLEDGE, UNDERSTANDING AND SKILLS

This section provides explanatory notes and exercises for each of the types of document that appear in the OCR exams. The notes and exercises for each different exam unit are grouped together.

The exercises are similar to the tasks you will have to complete in the exams, with circled instructions at the top of each document similar to those in the exam papers.

Notes pages

Notes pages precede each set of exercises. They explain how you should lay out documents and how to deal with the editing instructions. Take the time to read and understand the notes relating to each set of exercises before attempting them. You can refer to the notes as you work through each exercise.

Practice exercises

There are three new practice exercises for each type of document. Recall text for these exercises is available on the Hodder Plus website (see below). Once you have completed an exercise, proofread it and correct any errors. Save it using the filename indicated and print a copy. Find the correct worked example of the exercise in Chapter 5 and proofread your copy against this. If you are a member of a group, you may find it helpful to proofread each other's work.

Recall text from the Hodder Plus website

You will need to access files on the Hodder Plus website at www.hodderplus.co.uk/ocrtextprocessing to carry out the following:

- insert files for letter, memo, press release and file note headings files
- recall text to insert into your files
- access dictation for the audio-transcription exercises and practice exams.

To access these files you will need to enter the following username and password: **username:** text processing **password:** recall1

The templates that you will need to recall for Text Production and Audio-Transcription are saved under the following filenames:

LETTERHEAD   MEMO
FILE_NOTE   PRESS_RELEASE

For the purpose of these exercises and practice exams, you may use the same letterhead for any of the Text Production or Audio-Transcription documents, although some of the worked examples may show different letterheads. The same applies to the other templates, where slight variations may occur.

The letterhead templates with autotext and the recall text for Word Processing are saved under the filenames given in the exercises and practice exams documents.

Audio-Transcription

The Candidate Information Sheets (containing proper nouns) and Instruction to Invigilator Sheets (with information for document 3) are provided in this section. Dictated material is saved under filenames given to each exercise and accessed from the Hodder Plus website at **www.hodderplus.co.uk/ocrtextprocessing**.

TEXT PRODUCTION LEVEL 2 PRACTICE EXERCISES

WITH DETAILED NOTES ON HOW TO WORK THE FOLLOWING DOCUMENTS:

- Letter
- Memo
- Press release
- File note
- Report
- Article

LETTERS

Layout and style of a business letter

You will be required to produce a business letter in each of the Text Production, Word Processing and Audio-Transcription exams. For these exercises, a letterhead template will be provided on the Hodder Plus website. The font style, size and position of this must be retained. The body of the text may be in a different font, but must be easy to read – Arial 11 and Times New Roman 12 are popular.

Open punctuation is used in all OCR exams and in these exercises. This means that punctuation is inserted only where essential (e.g. full stops, apostrophes) or to clarify meaning (e.g. commas, brackets, dashes). Copy the punctuation given in the draft, but look out for missing full stops or superflous or misplaced apostrophes in the Text Production letter.

The sample letter that follows is in blocked style (each line starting at the left margin), apart from the letterhead, and is in open punctuation. This is the style used in OCR exams. There should be at least one clear linespace between each separate item, with equal spacing between paragraphs.

Date

You must date each letter with the date on which you take the exam. No instruction will be given in the draft, but a reminder is given on the front cover of the question paper. A good position for the date is before or after the reference, although other positions are acceptable. The following styles are all acceptable:

10 August 2009 10th August 09 August 10 2009 10 Aug 09 10.8.09

The example that is all in figures is more suitable for forms. In this style of date, if the month is shown before the day (i.e. 8.10.09), a penalty will be incurred, as it could be read as 8 October 2009.

Reference

Our ref must be displayed as shown in the draft. Follow the spacing, punctuation and capitalisation when keying in the actual reference. Do not add your initials to a reference, or add a *Your ref*, as this will incur a penalty.

Special mark

In the Text Production and Audio-Transcription exams, you have to key in a special mark. This is used to show special treatment of the document (e.g. *By Hand, Urgent* or *Private and Confidential*). If you place it immediately before the name and address of the recipient, it is less likely to be omitted when addressing an envelope or label, and it can be seen clearly through a window envelope. Follow the capitalisation given in the draft.

Name and address

Follow draft with regard to capitalisation. If the recipient's first name is drafted in full, that is how it should be keyed. Substituting an initial would be penalised.

Usual business practice is to show the name of the town in closed capitals, with the name of the county in initial capitals. In OCR exams and these exercises, abbreviations for *Drive, Street, Crescent*, and so on, should be expanded, but the county may remain abbreviated. The postcode should be keyed with one space between its two parts. It may appear on a separate line, or on the same line as the town/county and separated from it by several spaces, as shown below:

Mr Sane Khor
Computer Courses
MANCHESTER   M5 2JT

Salutation and complimentary close

The salutation and complimentary close need to follow business practice. Do not mix the styles – *Dear Sir* should not be followed by *Yours sincerely*, but always by *Yours faithfully.* The styles should match, as shown below:

Dear Sir(s)/Madam …   Yours faithfully
Dear Sane/Mr Khor …   Yours sincerely

Leave at least four clear linespaces for the signature. If the letter runs into a second page, then at least two lines of text should be carried over to the continuation sheet, along with the complimentary close.

Enclosure(s)

If the text indicates that an item/items are being enclosed, attached or included, you must show this at the end of the letter. Any appropriate methods are acceptable, but you must show clearly whether there are single or multiple enclosures. For example:

Enc/Encs   enc/encs   ENC/ENCS   Att/Atts   ATT/ATTS

Copies and routing

In OCR Word Processing and Audio-Transcription exams and exercises you must provide two extra copies of the letter, showing the destination and routing on each copy. The most straightforward method is to key all the details at the bottom of the original copy and show the routing on copies 1 and 2, as follows:

Original	*1st copy*	*2nd copy*
Copy Eddie Lanteri	Copy Eddie Lanteri √	Copy Eddie Lanteri
File	File	File √

You may prefer to tick the copies manually using a pen (not pencil), or by highlighting, emboldening or underlining. It is not essential for the details to appear on the original copy. This is called a *blind copy*, when these details only appear on the extra copies.

Continuation sheet

Where the letter goes on to a second page, that page should be printed on plain A4 paper. It should also be numbered, but no other details need appear, apart from your candidate name and centre number.

letterhead of writer	**Progress Group** **Westwood Way** **COVENTRY** *CV4 8JQ* **024 7647 0033**
Date letter prepared	20 August 2009
Writer's reference	Our ref AC/jpd/L208
Receiver's reference	Your ref SK/098
Special mark	URGENT
Name & address of person to whom the letter is written	Mr Sane Khor Computer Courses MANCHESTER M5 2JT
Salutation	Dear Mr Khor
Subject heading	TEXTBOOK ORDER KME L208
Paragraphs of text	Thank you for your order for the sets of the revised edition of Keyboarding Made Easy, which will be available in bookshops next week. I have arranged for the copies to be dispatched to you by DPL. I trust this will meet your deadline. In the meantime, I am enclosing an advance copy, for your personal use. You mentioned in your email that you are starting a new business course. You may find our current catalogue of interest, a copy of which is also enclosed. There is an excellent range of packages covering subjects such as the Internet, desktop publishing, databases and spreadsheets. Thank you for your custom and do not hesitate to contact us if we can be of further assistance.
Complimentary close	Yours sincerely
Space for signature of sender	
Name of sender Job title	April Chaplin Sales Executive
Enclosure(s) indicated	Encs
Person to receive copy	Copy Eddie Lanteri File

Amendments to text in letter document

Alterations to text

Refer to page 9 in the Assessment Criteria section of this book for the list of amendment and correction signs from the Text Production Syllabus. Some of these will appear in the following exercises.

Abbreviations and spellings

Abbreviations must be identified and expanded, and spelling errors identified and corrected. None of these will be circled at this level. The lists of abbreviations and spellings given on pages 9 and 10 of the Text Production Syllabus in Chapter 2 contain the only words that will be tested in this way in this unit.

Apostrophe and punctuation errors

The apostrophe error will be circled for you to correct. It will be either misplaced or superfluous.

The punctuation error for you to identify and insert could include an omitted full stop or initial capital, but the position will not be circled.

Grammatical errors

The errors of agreement will be circled and must be corrected. They will be very obvious at this level, e.g. *they is available*, *nine town*.

Postdating

There will be an instruction to provide a date for a precise day in the following month. In the main text, only the day and month need be inserted, as you do not need the year. For example, '. . . Our meeting on Monday 3rd August in Coventry'. The style used must be consistent throughout the document and should be the same style as the letter date.

Underlining

Text should be underlined as indicated in the draft.

EXERCISE TP 2.1

Our ref WB/hm

Mr K Rowe
10 Sherwood Ave
CALNE
Wiltshire
SN11 3GE

Mark this PRIVATE AND CONFIDENTIAL

Dr Mr Rowe

Thank you for coming into this ~~branch~~ ~~bank~~ to discus a ✓
bank loan. As agreed the money will be paid
into your current account on Wednesday
give date for the first Wednesday of next month
and you will be able to withdraw this money
the following day.

Repayments will be in six (instalment) and will be
taken directly from your account. I (has)
pleasure in enclosing ~~details and other particulars~~
~~for~~ the repayment plan. Please contact me if you
have any questions about your loan.

take this opportunity to
I would like to give you details about our range of
credit cards. The interest rate on all our credit (card's)
is very low. As well as paying for miscellaneous
items using your credit card you can also obtain
cash. As you are an existing customer and you
are in emp you would be able to get a credit
card very quickly. It is poss to transfer all of
your outstanding balances from other credit and
store cards in order to pay a lower interest rate.
If you would like any further info please let me
know. Thank you for your custom in the past. I look
forward to meeting you again in the future

Yrs sincerely

Wendy Barlow
Loan Manager

EXERCISE TP 2.2

Our ref   TR/SPT

Mrs R Walters
54 Main St   Mark this BY HAND
CHIEVELEY
RG17 6PG

Dr Mrs Walters

Thank you for your cheque for £100 which is the deposit
for your daughter's forthcoming school trip to Spain. I
enclose a receipts. Please note that the balance of £250
is due on Monday give date for last Monday of next month.

As discussed at our recent mtg, I confirm that group
members' will meet in the school hall on the day before
departure so that travel documents can be checked by
members of staff. A coach have been hired to take
everyone to the airport so there is no need for parents
to be concerned about transport. On our return, the
coach will bring everyone back to school. You are warmly
invited to collect your daughter and meet the other
parents. We will let you know our time of arrival. The
✓ staff believe that this visit will be very beneficial to all
students, particularly those who are getting ready for
their final examinations. It will offer learners the
chance to put their language skills into practice They
will /experience Spanish culture at first hand.
    also be able to

I am sure that your daughter will enjoy herself and I
would like to take this opp to thank you for your
financial support.

Yrs sncly

Toni Ramirez
Head of Languages

EXERCISE TP 2.3

Our ref JG/AB

Mr P McNaughton
246 Chaucer Sq
Intwood Park
NORWICH
NR4 7YZ

Mark this BY HAND

Dr Mr McNaughton

This is to confirm our tel conversation this morning. As disscused, we will start work on your art studio on Monday (give date for first Monday of next month).

Building regulations (requires) an inspection of the foundations. Weather permitting, we will aim to dig these out ready for approval on the Tues. Hardwood doors and window (frames') can be measured up ~~and ordered at this time~~ once the bricks have been laid. An order for the woodwork can then be put in.

✓ For ~~security~~ *safety* reasons we plan to complete all the external work before taking down the existing wall between your entrance porch and the new building.

We estimate that, *from start to finish,* the work will take about 6 (week). Meanwhile you can think about choosing the fixtures and fittings. Once the concrete floor and plasterwork have fully dried out, the room can be decorated with your choice of paint and emulsion. Worktops, cupboards, shelves, etc can then be fitted. [As agreed, you will make direct payment to the plumber and electrician   An allowance for this was shown on the estimate sent to you earlier this yr.

We look forward to completing this work to our usual high standard and on time.

Yours sncly

Jack Gorringe
Site Manager

MEMO/PRESS RELEASE/FILE NOTE

Layout and style

Templates are provided for these documents on the Hodder Plus website at www.hodderplus.co.uk/ocrtextprocessing. Add the details provided in the draft against the relevant headings. It is particularly important to check that the *To* and *From* details in the memo are against the correct headings, as they are not always drafted in the same order. The following styles are acceptable:

Leaving equal spaces	*Leaving unequal spaces*	*Using tab stop*
TO Mary White	**TO** Mary White	**TO** Mary White
FROM Peter Smith	**FROM** Peter Smith	**FROM** Peter Smith

Use the mouse or cursor keys to move between headings, to avoid creating extra linespaces. Do not add punctuation after the headings or infill details.

Date

Each of this type of document must be dated. In these exercises, no instructions to date the documents are given on the draft, but in a live exam a reminder will be given on the front cover of the question paper.

Amendments to text

Refer to page 9 in Chapter 2 for the list of amendment and correction signs from the Text Production Syllabus. Some of these will appear in these exercises.

Abbreviations and spellings

Abbreviations must be identified and expanded, and spelling errors identified and corrected. None of these will be circled at this level. The lists of abbreviations and spellings given on pages 9 and 10 of the Text Production Syllabus in Chapter 2 contain the only words that will be tested in this way in this unit.

Apostrophe and punctuation errors

The apostrophe error will be circled for you to correct. It will be either misplaced or superfluous.

There will be a punctuation error such as an omitted full stop or initial capital for you to identify and insert, but the position will not be circled.

Grammatical errors

The errors of agreement will be circled and must be corrected. They will be very obvious at this level, e.g. *they was going*, *many tree are*.

Enclosure(s)

In Text Production, an enclosure(s) may be indicated in the memo but not the press release or file note. The same rules apply as those given for business letters.

EXERCISE TP 2.4

Typist/operator: this is the memorandum

To   All Department Heads

From   Martin Perry, Office Manager

Ref   MP/hs

Next month there will be a health and safety inspection, so please ref to the booklet I sent to you last yr for the details.

One of my main concerns is items left in corridors. As you know there is a large storage area in the basement. if you need the keys to the basement I will arrange to let you have acess.

of equipment and furniture

The enclosed form requires your signature. The form states that by the end of the month you will act on this so please let me know if you have any questions.

EXERCISE TP 2.5

Typist/operator: this is a memorandum

From   Tom Brennan

To   Matt Robinson

Ref   TB/JEN

Keeps losing its satellite channels and

Mrs Jenkins of 15 Brackley Cres has been in touch with us again. Her 32 inch plasma television needs further attention. This is the third time she has contacted us recently. The television cannot be re-tuned automatically. Our (engineers') cannot resolve the problem.

I have spoken to Roger and we have agreed that the best way forward is to recall the television and return it to the mfr. Mrs Jenkins is very happy with this decision. please ask Sanjay to deliver a replacement set tomorrow morning to her. All the details are in the cleint file.

EXERCISE TP 2.6

typist/operator: this is a memorandum

To   Amelia Ayton

From   James Ricard

Ref   JR/MSS

I received a telephone call from Julie Lardent this morning about her application for the administrative assistant vacancy in our a/cs section. It appears that the Job Description was not enclosed in the information pack we sent her last week. I suggest that we email her a copy today.

We have so far received a number of applications for this post. we should compile a shortlist of candidates' in the near future. Refs can then be taken up before the interviews are held.   A definate date must be set aside for these within the next two weeks.

as this will save time

EXERCISE TP 2.7

Typist/operator: this is a press release

Company Name Progress Department Store

Contact Person Beverly Ford
                Personnel Manager

Progress Department Store is pleased
to announce the opening of a new
store in Bristol.

As this store will be approx double
the size of the current one we will
need to employ more staff. we require
permanent staff and temperary staff
next season. We will start holding
interview's next week. Please tel
if you would like an application form.

Everyone is welcome to come to the opening.
There will also be many bargains and
we are sure with the help of our staff
the new store will be a great success.

where there will be many free gifts

EXERCISE TP 2.8

Typist/operator: this is a press release

Contact Person   Damyanti Pattni
                        Human Resources Assistant

Company Name   Progress Electronics

Progress Electronics is pleased to announce the planned construction (in South Wales) of a second factory).

The business has enjoyed a surge in popularity over recent years. Increased demand for its products has led to the decision to expand the co's workforce. it is beleived the new building will be ready in two (year's) time. Approx 500 staff will be employed on the new site.

In response to this news, City analysts predict that Progress Electronics will continue to lead the way. As a result, share prices have risen by 15 per cent.

in Britain's fast-moving and innovative electronics industry

EXERCISE TP 2.9

typist/operator: this is a press release

Company Name   Progress Banking Group

Contact Person   Christa Weiss

Progress Banking Group is delighted to announce the launch of two new internet only accounts. These will be offered (with immed effect) to personal customers.

The online saver account can be opened with as little as £1. A fixed rate of interest is gnteed for the first year.

The other new online account is a cash individual savings account. this is tax free and may be opened with £10. (Customer's) can save up to £3,600 each year free of tax.

Both new accounts provide greater conveinence and flexibility. The environment should benefit as well.

and will help to reduce paper and postage

EXERCISE TP 2.10

Typist/operator: this is a file note

From   Jennifer Poole
Position   Customer Services Manager
File Number 2027

Mrs Brooke bought conservatory blinds from this co last year. We gave a gntee that the blinds would last for five years.

My secretary recieved a message on Friday last week from Mrs Brooke to say that one of her blinds was broken. I sent one of our inspector's to look at the problem. His report states that the fault is due to a badly stitched seam.

We will have to give Mrs Brooke a new blind but at present we do not have fabric available. in the colour to match

i have asked the quality control manager to review procedures.

EXERCISE TP 2.11

Typist/operator: this is a file note

From   Rekha Patel
Position   Training Manager
File Number   428

Todays' meeting with the External Verifier went very well. Jackie was extremely complimentary about the standard of work submitted. We will receive a copy of her report within the next few days.

the examinations board is planning to make some changes to the syllabus. Jackie has given us a copy of the new requirements. I intend to add this topic to the agenda for next week's meeting. We need to be clear how the changes will affect our org.

If poss, before we meet please look at the documents so that a full disscussion can take place.

All our portfolios were accepted.

EXERCISE TP 2.12

typist/operator: this is a file note

File Number   61189

From   Gemma Porter

Position   Office Manager

I spoke to Les Thompson, Recycling Officer, at County Hall with regard to collecting the furniture which is surplus to our requirements. He said that this would be poss. The collection day is a Wed in our area. He asked us to make sure the item's were left safely in full view before 7am on the day in question.

I explained that we were expecting delivery of some new equipment. upon reciept, we would request a collection date. He said they must have at least two weeks' notice.

I agreed to contact him in due course.

, for a small charge per item,

REPORT/ARTICLE

Layout and style

This document should be printed on plain A4 paper and has been designed to run on to two pages. It is not essential to number the first page, but the number must appear on the continuation sheet. To customise your page numbering, use **Insert → Page Numbers**.

Linespacing

Linespacing before and after headings and between paragraphs must be consistent within a document. You will be instructed to change the linespacing of a section of the text.

Headings

Follow the draft regarding capitalisation of headings. Leave at least one clear linespace before and after headings consistently. A heading should not be on a different page to the start of its related paragraph.

Amendments to text

Refer to page 9 in Chapter 2 for the list of amendment and correction signs from the Text Production Syllabus. Some of these will appear in these exercises.

Abbreviations and spellings

Abbreviations must be identified and expanded, and spelling errors identified and corrected. None of these will be circled at this level. The lists of abbreviations and spellings given on pages 9 and 10 of the Text Production Syllabus in Chapter 2 contain the only words that will be tested in this way in this unit.

Typographical errors

These are words containing extra, omitted and transposed letters and extraneous symbols. These are not circled at this level, but must be identified and corrected.

Grammatical errors

The errors of agreement will be circled and must be corrected. They will be very obvious at this level, e.g. *she were*, *two student*.

Emphasising text

You will be instructed to emphasise a portion of text. This is usually carried out by emboldening, using closed capitals or changing the font style/size. Make sure that you emphasise only the section indicated.

Distraction element

A sheet containing extra paragraphs of text for insertion into these documents is included with this exercise. It is important that you do not forget to key them in, as you will be penalised 1 mark for each omitted word.

EXERCISE TP 2.13

typist/operator: extra paragraphs for this document will be handed to you by the invigilator during the course of the examination

double linespacing except where indicated

PROGRESS COTTAGE HOLIDAYS

Cottage holidays provide the best value for money. Some of our cottages are available for rent all yr and some only during the summer months. We have all types of property on our books.

You can choose flats in city centres or charming country houses. What ever the size of your party we have acommodation to suit you.

in houses, chalets and cottages

Dogs is welcome but in some cases there is a limit to the number of dogs allowed so please check when booking. Properties with fenced gardens are very suitable for ~~dogs~~ and in our cat we have listed all ✓ these properties in one section.

Discounts for Next Season

emphasise this sentence

At the present time we are giving a discount for early bookings for next season. If you book two week with us you will recieve a free gift.

Holidays by the Sea or in Rural Areas

Adults and children like the beach. We have many chalets close to the sea and these are very popular with young families.

On our books
~~In addition to the chalets by the sea~~ we have cottages in rural areas and if you enjoy nature, some of these properties will provide you with the perfect holiday.

walking, playing and sitting on

<u>More Houses Needed</u>

We require more houses to rent asap. Please contact us immed if you can help.

(typist/operator: insert extra paragraphs here)

Some of our owners have more than one cotttage to let. In many areas in this country landlords can make more money with holiday lettings than they can with residential letings.

If you would like more detials about letting your property we will be pleased to talk to you. Alternatively, you can go to our website where you will find further information.

We insist that clients take out insurance to cover accidental damage when staying in holiday homes. This policy has beeen written for us by an insurance company. Therefore we know that the cover is enough to protect our owners from any loss.

It is hard for an owner to let property without any help. We do all the advertising and we collect the deposits and other payments from clients.

typist/operator: these are the extra paragraphs for the article

these paragraphs only in single linespacing

At Progress owners are paid good rates for holiday rentals. All we ask in return is that you keep the propert6y maintained.

Owners have to arrange for cleaning to be carried out each week and all the gardens must be kept tidy.

We look after everyone of our owners as we rely on them to provide an excelent service to our clients.

EXERCISE TP 2.14

Typist/operator: an extra paragraph for this document will be handed to you by the invigilator during the course of the examination

double linespacing except where indicated

PROGRESS GARDEN CENTRES

Progress Garden Centres have been in business since 1985 when Jean and Jack Denman started to develope their land as a nursery.

Over the years, helped by their familly and staff, the firm has grown. There are now nine garden centre across the West Midlands. Wherever you live within the region, you will not be far from one of our garden centres.

ADVICE AND GUIDANCE
Emphasise this sentence

are grown on our premises. They

From the outset Progress Garden Centres have been synonymous with quality. Healthy plants and shrubs are offfered for sale at competitive prices. Attractive displays show just how easily the plants can be grown. More unusual species are improted from Europe.

PLANTS AND SHRUBS

all experienced garden experts. They are

customers

Our staff are always happy to offer advice and guidance to clients. If you has a question, feel free to ask any member of staff as you wander around the centre. If the member questioned does not have an immed answer, we will contact you with the response asap.

LECTURE PROGRAMME

Typist/operator: insert extra paragraph here

These paragraphs only in single linespacing

GARDEN DESIGN

Running in conjunction with the nursery side of the business, we also run a garden design service. Our team of garden designers are fully qualified and have many years of experience between them.

If you wish to redesign your garden we can help. An initial visit to your garden and a full discussion of your ideas is offered free of charge. We will prepare a design and present it to you. If you like what we sugest, our design team will constr%uct the garden on your behalf, under taking the landscaping and planting for you. Prices start at £2000 for a small garden.

If you want to be fully involved in the transformation of your garden but need asistance with the planning process, we can work with you to produce plans. If you wish, we can draw up a planting diagram for you. This inexpencive service costs only £250 for an average garden.

CONTACT US

If you would like to visit one of our centres or use our garden design service, please visit our website: www.progressgardens.co.uk. We look forward to mtg you!

Typist/operator: this is the extra paragraph for the article

Every Friday morning, our garden experts give lectures ~~Once a week talks are delivered by centre staff~~ on a range of horticultural subjects. Each lecture lasts for approx one hour and is free of charge. However, as our lecture rooms are quite small, please book in advance. You can do this by calling your nearest Progress Garden Centre or by going to our website and following the link.

EXERCISE TP 2.15

typist/operator: extra paragraphs for this document will be handed to you by the invigilator during the course of this examination

double linespacing except where indicated

YAREDALE PROTECTION SOCIETY

The folllowing draft will form the basis of the Chairman's report at next month's meeting.

FUTURE PROJECTS IN YAREDALE

Our numbers (has) now dropped to around 300 households. Approx half of these are life members; 30% have paid for 5 years and the rest pay their subscriptions annually.

PUBLIC LIABILITY INSURANCE

After a long debat4e it was agreed that public liability insurance should be taken out. This would cover us for guided walks along the valley and for any social functoins that might be arranged during the year. It would also cover our Annual General Meeting.

MEMBERSHIP

Concern was expressed at the planning application for building 2 wind turbine in a lovely part of the valley. The society has no objection in principle to saving energy by building windfarms. However, the siting of such a developement is of prime importance. A number of petitions from other groups *, opposed to the project,* had been sent in. As a result the request was withdrawn.

It was noted that plannning permission for a leisure centre and retail outlet on land running down to the river had been refused.

emphasise this sentence

, although costly for a group such as ours,

YAREDALE WALKS BOOKLET

The committee agreed to update the current guide which hd sold well. ~~To date over 500 copies of the edition have been bought.~~ *This would include the new board (walk to the west of Yaredale.* It is hoped to publish the new guide early next year. Advertisers will be approached to help offset some of the cost.

NEWSLETTERS

The Chairman expressed his thanks to Patsy Smith for overseeing the distribution of the newsletters. Once again the question of sending these online was brought up. However, it was agreed to continue to deliver them by hand for the time being.

typist/operator: insert extra paragraphs here

WEBSITE

The society is ~~delighted~~ *pleased* to report that it now has a website. This includes some beautiful photgraphs of the valley taken during each season. New members can complete the membership form online. A token of apreciation has been sent to the designer.

Please email your comments to the Chairman asap.

typist/operator: these are the extra paragraphs for the report

these paragraphs only in single linespacing

CORRESPONDENCE

Several members have written to say that the footpath along the river is often flooded after heavy rain. Another member expressed concern over the amount of litter lying near the picnic tables close to the marshes.

The Sec has emailed the council about these matters.

Other correspondence received pointed out the danger of giant hogweed which has become a problem in the valley.

Planning info about new housing projects close to the river has also been received.

WORD PROCESSING LEVEL 2 PRACTICE EXERCISES

WITH DETAILED NOTES ON HOW TO WORK THE FOLLOWING DOCUMENTS:

- Article
- Information sheet
- Report
- Notice
- Poster
- Advertisement
- Table
- Letter

ARTICLE/INFORMATION SHEET/REPORT

Margins

In these exercises and the Word Processing exam you will be instructed to adjust the top and left margins of the document. Open the recall text, then use **File → Page Setup** to adjust the margins. Make sure that *Apply to Whole Document* is flagged. Highlight the text using **Control + A** and click the **Justify** icon. Ensure your margins are correct and start your text at the top of the page.

Header and footer

You will be instructed to insert a header or footer in this document. Use **View → Header and Footer** and use the toggle switch to move from one to the other. Key in the text and use the alignment icon to place it correctly.

Amendments to text

Refer to page 20 in Chapter 2 for the list of amendment and correction signs from the Word Processing Syllabus. Some of these will appear in these exercises.

Insetting text

When insetting a portion of text it is important that the measurement is exact.

To inset from the left margin, mark the relevant text and use **Format → Paragraph** and then the arrows in the left margin box to increase the paragraph indent.

Move and copy text

These are two distinct instructions and it is important that you understand the difference.

To **Move** a section of text use the **Cut** and **Paste** icons. The portion of text should appear only once in the document.

To **Copy** a section of text use the **Copy** and **Paste** icons. The portion of text should then appear twice in the document.

Find and replace

You will be required to change three instances of a recurring specified word in the document. Once all the text has been keyed, use **Edit** → **Replace**, complete the **Find What** and the **Replace With** boxes with the appropriate words and click **Replace All**.

Page breaks and numbering

This can be left to the end of the exercise. To insert page breaks, position your cursor where you wish to start a new page and use **Control + Enter**. This formatting can be deleted by using the Show/Hide icon (¶) to reveal the page break instruction, selecting *page break* and pressing **Delete**.

To insert page numbers, using **Insert** → **Page Numbers** will let you fully customise your numbering. **View** → **Header and Footer** can also be used.

Where indicated, the page number must not appear on page 1. This can be achieved by setting up a 'different first page' header and footer, which you will find on the layout tab of the page setup option. Ensure any text you have been asked to enter into the header/footer area appears on this page as well.

EXERCISE WP 2.1

> Recall the article stored as FRANCHISE. Amend as shown. Change to double linespacing (except where indicated). Adjust left margin to 4cm and the top margin to 5cm. Use full justification. Save as FRANCHISE2 and print one copy.

CHOOSING A FRANCHISE

a term which is

[Inset this paragraph 5cm from left margin]

Franchising is/used to describe a type of business arrangement which is becoming increasingly popular ~~in the United Kingdom~~. It involves the granting of a licence by one person (the franchisor) to another (the franchisee). This entitles the franchisee to ∧sell identical products or provide identical services.

With careful research a franchisee can become involved with a well-known brand at relatively low cost.

> Copy this sentence to point marked Ⓐ

trade under the brand established by the franchisor and to

THE ADVANTAGES

This arrangement is ideal for people who would like to run their own business but do not have the funds. A good franchise will offer a proven business format, along with instruction and support from the out set.

Investment costs range from as little as £5,000 for a share in a cleaning service *to £250,000 for a franchise in a major fast food outlet.*

The new investor will use (proven systems) [the same] as the main business, since these have been tried and tested. Therefore, the risks are fewer and the costs are much lower.

> Page 2 starts here

Ⓑ

Continuing instruction will be given to ensure that the brand quality is up held and the business remains profitable.

 Ⓐ

> Or the experience to go it alone

> Insert BUSINESS OPTIONS to appear as a footer at the right margin on every page

> Change instruction to guidance throughout this document

Move to point marked Ⓑ

When the agreement is finalised, the franchisee will often spend time working alongside the franchisor, to see exactly how the business works. Training will usually be given to improve knowledge and skill.

THE DISADVANTAGES

As with any business that is not entirely one's own, many Franchisees feel frustrated that they cannot put their own stamp on the business.

This section only in single linespacing

complete allegiance

However, part of the agreement compels ~~total adherence~~ to the proven way of working, from the design of uniforms to the components used in the manufacturing process. [Another consideration, after the initial financial investment, is the payment of fees on the profits made. Whilst the franchise agreement is in force, the franchisee is compelled to pay fees to the franchisor.

✓

EUROPEAN CODE OF ETHICS FOR FRANCHISING

The European Franchise Federation (EFF) was set up to promote the franchise industry in general and its members' interests in particular.

consultation with franchise organisations in 10 European countries

In 1989, after ~~speaking to delegates across Europe~~, it reviewed its Code of Ethics. *This exists to support the ethical conduct of all business relating to franchising and is a useful source of reference for those who involve themselves in a franchise agreement.*

Page 3 starts here

MORE INFORMATION

To learn more about franchising

~~If you want to find a franchise partner~~, contact the British Franchise Association. They offer free advice and instruction on how to get the best out of setting up a franchise opportunity. Check out their website for ways to limit your risk!

Number the pages, ensuring that Page 1 is not numbered

EXERCISE WP 2.2

Recall the article stored as ROTATION. Amend as shown. Change to double linespacing (except where indicated). Adjust left margin to 5 cm and the top margin to 7.5 cm. Use full justification. Save as CROPS and print one copy.

and to control contamination by pests and diseases

CROP ROTATION

Farmers have always followed the practice of crop rotation. This is a scheme of regularly changing the crops grown on a piece of land. The crops are grown in a particular order to utilise and add to the nutrients in the soil.

A typical rotation may consist of grass or potatoes followed by a wheat crop and then one of barley. In this way, the cereal crops take advantage of the build-up of soil fertility which occurs during the period under grass. The quality of the ground dictates whether there will be one or two crops of wheat and barley.

Inset this paragraph 4.5 cm from left margin

In modern farming, the potato or grass crop may be replaced with a forage crop such as maize. The heavy use of manure required for this crop ensures that two crops of wheat and two crops of barley can be grown easily in following years.

Move to point marked ■

Gardeners can follow the same principles of crop rotation when growing vegetables. Follow the basic rule of not planting the same crop in the same place for more than one year at a time.

Page 2 starts here

definitely benefit from being grown

Vegetables certainly thrive when planted in soil that has not been used for the same crop the previous year.

Copy this sentence to point marked ▲

Different plants need different growing conditions so soil type needs to be established. It is important to distinguish between the acid or alkaline content.

Change scheme to system throughout this document

because it will not be rotated each year

This section only in single linespacing

to ensure optimum growth and yield

Decide ~~before planting~~ on the conditions needed for each crop. Some crops prefer a neutral to acid soil *whereas others thrive in an alkaline soil.*

The beds should be dug over thoroughly and fertilised. Lime should be added to produce the correct alkaline level.

Page 3 starts here

four beds

Divide the growing area into ~~several sections~~. Some crops such as rhubarb, strawberries, raspberries, all fruit trees and asparagus can be grown each year in the same position. The area where these crops will be planted will be a permanent bed. It should be thoroughly prepared before planting.

remaining three beds would become

The ~~rest of the area can be~~ part of a simple rotation. ▲

For the first year, root crops such as carrots, beetroot and parsnips can be planted in the first bed.

In the second year, this bed would contain potatoes and tomatoes. In the third year, cabbages, cauliflowers, broccoli and sprouts could be planted. Gardeners often have limited space available so this simple rotation scheme is effective. With more space, the rotation scheme can be extended to four or five years. The longer the ground is given to recover between planting the same crop, the better the results will be.

Insert VEGETABLE PLANTING to appear as a header at the right margin on every page

Number the pages ensuring that Page 1 is not numbered

EXERCISE WP 2.3

Recall this report stored as SCHOOLS. Amend as shown. Change to double linespacing (except where indicated). Adjust left margin to 4.5 cm and the top margin to 6 cm. Use full justification. Save as SCHOOLS1 and print one copy.

SCHOOL PARTNERSHIPS

Over the last 3 years the company has

~~It had been considered important that the firm~~ developed a partnership with 5 local primary schools. Volunteers from our staff have been involved in a variety of initiatives. They have helped run activities such as vegetable gardening.

Jill Bacon co-ordinates the volunteers and liaises

~~Our Human Resource Department agreed to run this scheme~~ with the schools on a regular basis. It has been decided to continue these initiatives ~~on an informal basis~~. The response from our staff has been excellent.

the headmistress of Lower Middleton Primary,

Pip North, suggested that because of our expertise we might consider sponsoring buying a small greenhouse which could be used for propagation.

The pupils have tried in the past growing seeds but with little success. The school is sited on a very windy hill with poor soil and sowing seeds had been unsuccessful. The children have become disheartened. It was felt that it was important that the children see fairly fast results although also seeing failures. ← copy this sentence to point marked (A)

This section only in single linespacing

Page 2 starts here

FINANCE

The schools are very appreciative of the volunteers' help.

These school initiatives have been funded from the Partnership Fund. Any donations from staff are matched by the company. It has been agreed that the company will top up the Fund by £1000 which will cover the initial costs so that other sponsorships are not affected.

Move to point marked (B)

If any of the other schools want a greenhouse it should be possible to offer another 2 next year. It is hoped to gain valuable information from this project which can be used with the other schools.

VEGETABLES OR FLOWERS?

As part of their learning the children will take responsibility for deciding what crops to grow. Jill Bacon has contacted the local allotment society. The society has been very helpful. John Rivers, from the North Allotment Society, has produced a list of what should grow well. These include cabbages, courgettes, leeks, lettuce, peas, potatoes and radishes. (A)

(Page 3 starts here)

(Inset this section 3cm from left margin)

John has also produced a list which includes carrots and parsnips. He has agreed to be the school's vegetable consultant. This should be a useful contact for the school. Care must be taken in ensuring that the vegetables are not ready in the summer holidays so it is important to research suitable varieties. The care taker has agreed to do any watering that is required during weekends and holidays.

of what does not grow well in this area

FUTURE DEVELOPMENTS

(B)

SETTING UP

~~Jason Heath~~

The caretaker has agreed to liaise with the setting up of the greenhouse. *It has been decided to put in staging at different heights so that children from various age groups can use the greenhouse so gaining its full potential.*

(Insert Middleton School to appear as a footer at the right margin on every page)

(Change initiatives to projects throughout this document.)

(Number the pages ensuring that Page 1 is not numbered)

EXERCISE WP 2.4

> Recall the information sheet stored as BEDS. Amend as shown. Change to double linespacing (except where indicated). Adjust left margin to 5cm and the top margin to 6cm. Use full justification. Save as BEDS2 and print one copy.

SLEEP EASY WITH PROGRESS

With almost 20% of the population suffering from a lack of sleep, it makes sense to try to alleviate the problem by making some changes. Too much activity close to bed time can result in disrupted sleep patterns. A warm bath before bed may also be helpful.

> Alternatively, perhaps a change of bed is needed. That is where Progress can help!

> Copy this sentence to point marked Ⓐ

Our Progress showrooms stock a range of beds that can make a big difference to the quality of your sleep.

> For some people, a change in lifestyle is required.

TYPES OF BED

> This section only in single linespacing

You should be able to find one to suit your needs and your budget. Progress Beds come in 4 main sizes – single, double, queen (5 feet) and king (6 feet). Other widths can be ordered as necessary. Lengths vary too. The standard length is 6 feet, but an additional 6 inches is usual on king-sized beds. Very tall people often request an even longer bed.

> There are many different types and sizes of bed.

MATTRESSES

Sharing a bed with ~~a partner~~ your spouse does not necessarily mean that a mattress has to be shared too. Larger beds may have zipped mattresses. This means that each partner has a separate mattress (possibly of a different firmness) to suit their particular needs. The mattresses are zipped together but can be separated if one partner becomes ill.

> Page 2 starts here

Most of our clients are looking for a mattress which is comfortable and supportive. This will be different for everyone, since a person's height and build will determine which style is most suitable. The majority of our clients opt for a firm mattress.

The term 'orthopaedic' means extra firm and these for some people may be too hard. Foam mattresses are non-allergenic and do not need turning.

> Change clients to customers throughout this document

Move to point marked Ⓑ

Inset this paragraph 5 cm from left margin

CHOOSING YOUR NEW BED

A new bed is not a cheap purchase. It makes sense to keep your bed in good condition. In this way, it will last and be comfortable throughout its lifetime.

Ⓐ

to compare comfort and support

We recommend that our clients lie on a selection of beds in the showroom. If you share your bed, try out the beds together.

Look for a firm core support. This will hold your spine in correct alignment. A quilted surface will give better insulation.

Page 3 starts here

TAKING CARE OF YOUR BED

Ⓑ

Use a protective cover on your mattress and pillows. ~~Remove stains carefully and change bedlinen weekly.~~ Some covers protect against allergies. Vacuum your mattress and base occasionally to remove dust. Air your bed every day so that perspiration can evaporate and the bed stays fresh.

bed should give you years of comfortable sleep!

Careful attention to your ~~sleeping habits can result in much improved rest~~

Insert BEDS UPDATE to appear as a footer at the left margin on every page

Number the pages ensuring that Page 1 is not numbered

EXERCISE WP 2.5

Recall the information sheet stored as BALLOON. Amend as shown. Change to double linespacing (except where indicated). Adjust the left margin to 5.5 cm and the top margin to 6.5 cm. Use full justification. Save as BALLOON2 and print one copy.

HOT AIR BALLOONS

Copy this sentence to point marked ⊗

and actually took place as long ago as 1785

▶Ballooning is an activity that has inspired people to test their endurance and capabilities to the limit. The first crossing of the English Channel was undertaken by a Frenchman and his American co-pilot. During the early and middle parts of the last century, balloonists concentrated on setting altitude records.

In 1935 a new altitude record was set which remained unchallenged for 20 years. The balloon reached a height of 72,395 feet or 13.7 miles. The success of the attempt showed that humans could survive at this high altitude in a pressurised chamber. It provided invaluable data that was used in future space travel.

The quest for attaining the altitude record was followed by balloonists concentrating on distance and flight duration times. The Atlantic Ocean was crossed successfully followed a few years later by flights across the Pacific Ocean.

Move to point marked ▲

Companies frequently decide to use hot air balloons to advertise their products or services. It can be an effective form of advertising. The balloon can be made in a variety of shapes, sizes and colours.

Page 2 starts here

There have been several famous people who exploits seem ✓
Over the years many celebrities have taken part in these challenges. Their attempts appear to fire the public's imagination and their progress is watched avidly. ⊗

of a hot air balloon
The main parts of a balloon are the basket, envelope and burner. The basket carries the passengers, pilot and gas canisters.

It is made of woven cane which is fairly light in weight but at the same time is flexible and sturdy. This strength is needed as it has to withstand considerable force on landing.

Number the pages ensuring that Page 1 is not numbered

Inset this section 3.5 cm from the left margin

(Page 3 starts here)

There are two main types of basket

~~The design varies according to requirements~~. One is designed with compartments so that passengers can be separated from the pilot and cylinders. The other one has no compartments so the passengers, pilot and canisters are all housed together. The compartments allow the weight to be distributed evenly and this improves safety.

(This paragraph only in single linespacing)

The envelope is the actual balloon. The main part is made from the same material used for parachutes. Nylon is a reliable material because it is lightweight, strong and has a high melting temperature. The bottom part of the envelope is made from a ~~specially made~~ flame resistant material.

The burner propels the hot air up into the envelope so that the balloon can take off. Hot air balloons are based on the basic principle that hot air rises in cooler air. Propane gas is used in modern balloons. It is highly compressed in canisters and flows to the burner in liquid form.

It is a combination of nylon and polyester.

Insert PROGRESS BALLOONS to appear as a footer in the centre on every page

Change canisters to cylinders throughout this document

EXERCISE WP 2.6

Recall the information sheet stored as GREENHOUSES. Amend as shown. Change to double linespacing (except where indicated). Adjust left margin to 6.5 cm and the top margin to 5 cm. Use full justification. Save as GREENHOUSES1 and print one copy.

A GREENHOUSE

ADVICE ON CHOOSING YOUR LEAN-TO ✓

copy this sentence to point marked (Y)

You need to consider what you are going to use the greenhouse for. They can be used for propagating seeds and plants. They allow the gardener to extend the growing season so enabling you to grow flowers and vegetables earlier in the year. The general advice has been that you will always need a larger greenhouse than you think you need.

SHAPE

Generally modern greenhouses can be divided into 4 shapes

A wide range of designs are available. There is the lean-to. This is where one wall is formed by the house or other building and the green house leans on this wall. Unlike conservatories there is often no direct access to the interior of the house. They do not suffer because of the wall from temperature extremes. Usually it is easier to get electricity and water services to the lean-to.

The other common type is the apex

A ridge-style constitutes a typical greenhouse design. This is freestanding and has a pitched roof with parallel sides. The Dutch light greenhouse has sloping sides and the hexagonal type has angular sides.

Page 2 starts here

TYPE

The choice is usually between wood and aluminium. There are a variety of different types of wood such as pine, cedar, teak and oak. A range of timber may be used within the same greenhouse. Aluminium greenhouses require no maintenance. They do not rust. They are cheaper than wood but do not look as attractive. If the bolts and screws are made of steel these may corrode.

with new materials being developed

Timber greenhouses need to be repainted regularly. Alternatives such as polyethylene and acrylic are cheaper but short lived.

move this paragraph to point marked (▲)

There is a wide range such as horticultural glass, toughened glass or plastic glazing. Think about whether you need automatic vents. A closed greenhouse may heat up to tropical temperatures during the day.

Inset this paragraph 2.5cm from left margin

HEATING

Heating is expensive. Think about whether it is necessary to heat the whole of the greenhouse or only part of it. An alternative to heating is to have a heated propagator or propagators. This would require electrical sockets. Another option might be to have a very small heated greenhouse and a separate polytunnel.

Page 3 starts here

This section only in single linespacing

SIZE

choose a suitable size,

Having decided on this, to help you lay out each activity on your lawn. For example, if you want to grow tomatoes, put out the grow-bags required. It is usually better to have a wider greenhouse than a longer one as there will be less walkway and more growing space.

GLAZING

Remember to leave space down the middle for the walkway.

Time spent doing research before buying a greenhouse is time well spent.

Number the pages ensuring that Page 1 is not numbered

Insert Greenhouse Information to appear as a header at the left margin of every page

Change wood to timber throughout the document

NOTICE/POSTER/ADVERTISEMENT FOR DISPLAY

Landscape printing

In these exercises and the Word Processing exam this display document must be printed in landscape. To work in landscape format, make sure you are in *Print Layout View,* then use **File** → **Page Setup** → **Paper Size** and select **Landscape**.

Font size

You will be instructed to increase the font size of a selected portion of text. Just alter the size – do not alter the font style.

Amendments to text

Refer to page 20 in Chapter 2 for the list of amendment and correction signs from the Word Processing Syllabus. Some of these will appear in these display document exercises.

Inserting a picture

You will be told to insert a picture within the text, which you can recall from the Hodder Plus website, using the given filename.

To change the measurement as instructed:

- right click the picture → **Format Picture** → **Size**, then select measurement.

To arrange the word wrapping:

- right click the picture → **Format Picture** → **Layout**, select text wrapped to left or right of picture, as indicated in the draft.

Sorting a list

Use **Table** → **Sort** → **Ascending** or **Descending**. To sort text in alphabetical order, choose **Ascending**.

Automatic word count

To perform an automatic word count of this document, proofread and save it using the specified filename. Use **Tools** → **Word Count** and key the number of words specified at the bottom of the document. Save again.

EXERCISE WP 2.7

Recall the notice stored as ALPS. Amend as shown. Save as ALPS2. Print a copy in landscape on one sheet of A4 paper.

WALKING IN THE SWISS ALPS ← (Centre)

This paragraph only in a larger font size

Our next planned excursion will take place in June. We propose to travel by luxury coach to Switzerland. We will stay in a 4-star hotel in the beautiful town of Interlaken. From there we will arrange trips into the mountains. We will also organise walks in the foothills for those who are fit.

or relax in the warm sunshine

If you prefer not to walk, there are open air spas where you can swim. The excursion will last for nine days.

The cost of £350 per person includes seven nights' accommodation in Interlaken and one overnight stop in France on the outgoing and return journeys.

If you would like to reserve your place, please let us have details of your

Travelling companion
Nationality
Name and address
Phone number (mobile)
Passport

Sort into exact alphabetical order

as soon as possible.

Places are limited so don't delay. Book your place today!

A deposit of £100 per person will also be required.

On completion ensure you have saved your work and then use your software facilities to perform a word count. Key in this figure on a separate line below the final line of text.

Insert the picture here stored as CHALET. Change the measurement to 3.5 cm wide with the text wrapped to the left of the picture.

EXERCISE WP 2.8

Recall the Notice stored as SEEDS. Amend as shown. Save as SEEDS1. Print a copy in landscape on one sheet of A4 paper.

VOLUNTEERING AT LOWER MIDDLETON PRIMARY SCHOOL — Centre this heading

In time it is hoped to extend this project to other local primary schools.

As many of you know the Partnership Fund runs a gardening project with Lower Middleton Primary School.

Insert the picture here stored as PACKETS. Change measurement to 3cm wide with the text wrapped to the right of the picture.

A range of easy to grow varieties are needed which can be sown at different times of the year. To kick start the project if anyone has spare vegetable seeds please pass these on to Jill Bacon in Human Resources.

We particularly need seeds of:

Courgettes — This list only in a larger font size.
Cabbages
Lettuces
Leeks — Please sort into exact alphabetical order
Radishes
Peas
Potatoes

Come and meet other volunteers and find out more about the volunteering projects at the open evening which is being held on 26 October from 5.30 pm in the canteen.

Over 50 people volunteer on a regular basis. If you have little spare time, what about volunteering for our 2 big fundraising days in June and September?

Remember any money that is raised by the Partnership Fund is matched by the company.

On completion, ensure you have saved your work and then use your software facilities to perform a word count. Key in this figure on a separate line below the final line of text.

EXERCISE WP 2.9

Recall the poster stored as FLIGHT. Amend as shown. Save as FLIGHT2. Print a copy in landscape on one sheet of A4 paper.

BALLOON FLIGHTS

Experience the magic of a ride in a hot air balloon. Nothing can compare with floating gently over undulating countryside. Familiar landmarks look so different when viewed from above.

Where will your flight end? The destination is dictated solely by wind direction and speed.

Celebrate in style. Come on your own or with friends to share in this unique experience.

The items listed will contribute to a comfortable and memorable flight.

Warm clothing
Binoculars
Batteries for camera
Camcorder
Camera
Fleece
Flat footwear
Sunglasses

Sort into exact alphabetical order

Centre this section

The flight will last for around one hour. Be prepared that the landing maybe bumpy. Our pilot will ensure that discomfort is kept to a minimum. Passengers will be transported back to the starting point. Finish your special day with a celebratory glass of champagne!

This paragraph only in a larger font size

Insert the picture here stored as RIDE. Change measurement to 4cm wide with the text wrapped to the left of the picture.

do everything possible to
Progress Balloons undertakes to ensure that flights take place as scheduled. Adverse weather conditions may necessitate the cancellation of flights at short notice.

On completion ensure you have saved your work and then use your software facilities to perform a word count. Key in this figure on a separate line below the final line of text.

EXERCISE WP 2.10

Recall the advertisement stored as CLEANING. Amend as shown. Save as CLEANING2. Print a copy in landscape on one sheet of A4 paper.

CLEAN YOUR HOUSE THE PROGRESS WAY! ← Centre

If you are too busy to spend time cleaning your home, why not ~~take a break and~~ give Progress Cleaning Services a call? Our professional staff can visit weekly or monthly and will clean your house to an exceptional standard. Book online at www.progresscleaning.co.uk.

the following services

Our normal schedule includes:

Dust all surfaces
Clear away rubbish
Clean soft furnishings   Sort into exact alphabetical order
Polish mirrors
Vacuum carpets
Wipe down paintwork
Wash floors

This paragraph only in a larger font size

However, should you wish us to concentrate on a particular room or perform an 'intensive clean, we can undertake specific tasks. We charge by the hour and you can limit the time we spend in your home.

For a limited period only, we are delighted to offer new customers a 10% discount on their first booking.

So why not make a booking today?

Please email us if you would like to receive our informative booklet. Get in touch today.

On completion, ensure you have saved your work and then use your software facilities to perform a word count. Key in this figure on a separate line below the final line of text.

Insert the picture here stored as VACUUM. Change measurement to 3.5 cm wide with the text wrapped to the left of the picture.

EXERCISE WP 2.11

Recall the advertisement stored as SANDWICH. Amend as shown. Save as SAND2. Print a copy in landscape on one sheet of A4 paper.

PROGRESS SANDWICH BAR ← Centre this heading

We have established our reputation by using the best quality ingredients in our products.
We guarantee to provide the freshest sandwiches, rolls and baguettes.

Our bread is traditionally baked each day. We use free range eggs, vegetables and salad from our own smallholding. Our meat is supplied by a local farmer. All our suppliers are reputable.

of breads and fillings

We offer an extensive and imaginative choice. Tell us if you want something different. We can mix and match our ingredients to meet your requirements.

Insert here the picture stored as CHOICE. Change measurement to 6cm wide with the text wrapped to the right of the picture.

Here is a selection of items available daily.

Nourishing soups
Crisps and dips
Cheese flans
Sandwiches and baguettes
Sausage rolls
Tropical fruit platter
Traditional cakes

Sort into exact alphabetical order

This section only in a larger font size

Fruit such as apples, oranges and bananas can be purchased individually. For those with a sweet tooth, taste our mouth-watering pastries and desserts.

Telephone or fax 01884 661470 with your order and claim an introductory 20% discount.

Our new sandwich bar opens next Monday in Old Square.

On completion ensure you have saved your work and then use your software facilities to perform a word count. Key in this figure on a separate line below the final line of text.

EXERCISE WP 2.12

Recall the advertisement stored as SHOWGROUND. Amend as shown. Save as SHOWGROUND1. Print a copy in landscape on one sheet of A4 paper.

This heading only in a larger font size

FROM FEBRUARY 1 TO JULY 1 AT THE RIVERFIELD SHOWGROUND at the end of the field

(Turn left at the Beechwood traffic lights. There is plenty of parking.)

Consultants from Green Greenhouses will be available to offer advice on selecting the appropriate greenhouse and ancillary equipment.

There will be a permanent display of over 20 of the latest greenhouses.

The range includes contemporary designs. There are timber and aluminium greenhouses which are available in a wide range of sizes and shapes. A new hexagonal design is proving popular as it has very attractive features at a competitive price.

The majority of greenhouses have a choice of glazing from toughened or horticultural glass. There is the option to purchase automatic vents.

A range of chicken coops will also be on display.

Centre this line

The following greenhouse accessories will be on offer at a 25% discount.

Guttering
Horticultural fleece
Heaters
Seed trays
Solid staging
Slatted staging
Electric propagators
Watering cans

sort into exact alphabetical order

On completion, ensure you have saved your work and then use your software facilities to perform a word count. Key in this figure on a separate line below the final line of text.

Insert the picture here stored as APEX. Change measurement to 4 cm wide with the text wrapped to the right of the picture.

TABLE

Tables versus tabs

Although you may use preset or customised tabs when dealing with very simple table layouts, in Word Processing you need to use the table facility, as it will allow you to merge and insert cells, and move columns of text vertically and horizontally using the cut and paste icons.

Keying in

Key in across each horizontal line of words, using the tab key or mouse to reach each column or cell and inserting the necessary linespacing as you go, either by pressing **Enter** or **Table** → **Insert Row**. Once all the text has been keyed in, the document should be saved before you modify it. Then you do not incur so many penalties if you run out of time or lose blocks of text while editing.

Alignment of text

Block all text and figures in columns consistently to the left. Data in columns must be aligned with the column headings. Decimal points must be aligned, with the first figure of the longest number aligned with the column heading.

Column width and spacing between

Using the table method, it is simple to insert a table, choosing the number of columns you need and keeping the automatic column width. When keying in, let the text wrap round inside the cells, moving between them using the tab or cursor keys. To create more rows, make sure the cursor is in the last cell and press the tab key. Dragging columns to the correct width, merging and splitting cells should be the last editing options used, as they could interfere with selecting and moving text. The spacing between each column does not have to be equal, but a minimum of three spaces is a good rule.

Proofreading

This should be done before any text is moved or sorted, as it is much easier to check against the draft at this stage.

Modifying layout

In these exercises, you are instructed to change either the order of columns or the order of sections. Using the table method, this may be done through **Table** → **Select Column** or **Select Row** then using the cut and paste icons to insert the relevant text in its new position. This should not prove difficult as long as you have left sufficient space (**Insert Columns/Insert Rows**) in which to paste the selected text.

Merging and splitting cells

To allow a heading to spread over two or more columns, select the heading row and use **Table** → **Merge Cells**.

To divide columns/rows use **Table** → **Split Cells** → *select number of columns/rows.*

Sorting lists

In the Word Processing exam you are instructed to sort sections of text into alphabetical, numerical or chronological (date) order. It is best to make any changes in column order before carrying out a sort. Use the automatic sort option: **Table** → **Sort** → select **Text/Number/Date** → select **Ascending/ Descending**.

If you need to sort figures starting with the lowest, select **Ascending**. If you need to sort figures starting with the highest, select **Descending**.

Capitals

It is important that you follow the draft regarding capitalisation of headings and listed items, otherwise penalties will be incurred.

Ruling

It is easier to work with visible gridlines when keying a table. However, you are not required to show ruling in the exam. To remove the gridlines once you have completed the table, first select the table, then use **Format** → **Borders and Shading** → **Borders**, and under **Setting** select **None**.

Text before and after the table

In these exercises there will be text to insert both before and after the table. It is important that you remember to do this and to key in any additional hand-written text shown in the draft.

Vertical space

In print layout view, use the left-hand ruler to measure the space, which should be taken from the bottom of the last line of text to the top of the following text.

EXERCISE WP 2.13

Recall the document stored as COSTS. Amend as shown. Retain the Arial 11 font throughout the document. Save as COSTS2 and print one copy.

PROGRESS HOLIDAYS

In times of financial uncertainty, people look for ways to reduce costs, particularly at holiday times. If you have been worried about the costs of hiring holiday accommodation overseas, the following table will convince you that it is cheaper than you thought!

BOOKING OPTIONS	BOOKING CODE	FURTHER INFORMATION	
		PRE-BOOKING REQUIRED?	COST PER WEEK £
LUXURY VILLA ON COSTA DEL SOL			
Secluded villa to sleep 4 people	VAH1	Yes	960.00
Rental vehicle (4 days)	HCA9	No	89.70
Daily housekeeper	DHK6	Yes	240.00
Membership of health club	MMC8	No	100.00
BUDGET APARTMENT ON COSTA DEL SOL			
Apartment to sleep 4 people	APC1	Yes	276.00
Welcome food pack	WPF5	Yes	25.90
Regular cleaning service	DCS3	No	75.50
Use of beach hut	UBH2	No	20.00
Rental vehicle (4 days)	HCA9	No	89.70

The above prices include local taxes. All Progress properties enjoy the use of a pool and barbecue.

Leave a vertical space of at least 2.5 cm here

A 10% reduction is available for new customers.

Modify layout so that BUDGET APARTMENT ON COSTA DEL SOL section comes before LUXURY VILLA ON COSTA DEL SOL section

Please sort COST PER WEEK £ column into exact numerical order within each section starting with the highest number first. Ensure all corresponding details are also rearranged

EXERCISE WP 2.14

Recall the document stored as SNACK. Amend as shown. Retain the Arial 11 font throughout the document. Save as SNACK2 and print one copy.

Modify layout so that LOCATION OF STORE column becomes the last column

QUALITY FARE FROM PROGRESS

New sandwich recipes are being introduced in a selection of our stores. Our website www.progress.fare.co.uk gives full details of the location of these trial stores. Download a sample menu.

BREAD	CHOICE OF FILLING	COST AND AVAILABILITY	
		LOCATION OF STORE	RETAIL PRICE £
ASSORTED SANDWICH SELECTION			
Farmhouse	Mozzarella cheese with tomato and basil	Exeter	2.70
Wholemeal	Cream cheese with roasted vegetables	Taunton	2.95
Wheatmeal	Roast lamb with organic mint jelly	Bristol	3.75
Pitta	Steak with spicy horseradish relish	Bath	3.90
Ciabatta	Chargrilled vegetables	Taunton	2.65
Granary	Chicken breast with herbs and chutney	Bath	3.95
Wheatmeal	Bacon, lettuce and sun-dried tomatoes	Yeovil	3.25
SPECIALITY SANDWICH PLATTERS			
Farmhouse	Chicken and turkey with coriander salad	Bristol	15.75
Granary	Scottish smoked salmon, prawns and tuna	Barnstaple	16.50
Wheat-free	Selection of tasty regional cheeses	Chard	13.95

Leave a vertical space of at least 9 cm here

Telephone 01404 747033 with your order. Take advantage of our daily delivery service straight to your door.

Please sort RETAIL PRICE £ column into exact numerical order within each section starting with the lowest number. Ensure all corresponding details are also rearranged.

EXERCISE WP 2.15

> Recall the document stored as FEATURES. Amend as shown. Retain the Arial 11 font throughout the document. Save as FEATURES1 and print one copy.

NEW PRODUCTS

The latest catalogue will be available by the end of next month. You will see from the sample items listed below that our range is expanding into fruit and vegetables.

> Leave a vertical space of at least 6cm here

DESCRIPTION	SIZE	CODE AND WHOLESALE PRICE	
		STOCK NUMBER	PRICE (£)
GARDENING ACCESSORIES			
Vegetable planters	45 cm diameter	PP6	5.00
Insulating fleece	1000 cm long	FL7	9.25
Aluminium fruit cage	90 cm high	FC8	105.00
Strawberry tower	Holds 24	ST3	26.00
Micromesh tunnel cloche	90 cm long	BP2	30.00
ORNAMENTAL GARDEN FEATURES			
Decorative fruit cage	250 cm square	FC9	390.00
Willow obelisk	150 cm high	WW5	40.50
Obelisk pyramid	180 cm high	PP2	100.00
Pyramid cold frame	120 cm square	CF24	150.00
Victorian bell jar	Medium	VB7	25.50

Josie Holland is handling all suppliers' enquiries. She is sending out the catalogue to all our registered suppliers. If you do not receive it by the beginning of August or need any other help please ring her on 024 7647 0033.

> Modify layout so that ORNAMENTAL GARDEN FEATURES section comes before GARDENING ACCESSORIES.

> Please sort PRICE (£) column into exact numerical order within each section starting with the lowest first. Ensure all corresponding details are also rearranged.

LETTER

See the notes under Text Production (page 45) for detailed information on the layout of business letters. Unless stated otherwise, the same rules apply. However, you will not be tested on amendments to text in these Word Processing exercises.

Font style

In these exercises and in the Word Processing exam you will need to use a specified font style and size for the letter text. When selecting the specified font, make sure your cursor is positioned *after* the letterhead, so that you do not change the font style of the letterhead itself. You must use the specific font style for all of the letter apart from the letterhead.

Right margin

You will be instructed to use a justified or ragged right margin. This is best selected at the start of the document, using the **Align Left** or **Justify** icons.

Bullet points

Bullet points will be included in the letter. Make sure that the linespacing before and after the bulleted section is equal and that there is consistent spacing within the bullets.

Autotext

In the Word Processing exam you will be instructed to insert two phrases of autotext. They will be linked to the letterhead template, so you need to make sure you use the correct filenames to select each of them. Move your cursor to the point of insert, then use **Insert** → **AutoText** → key the stored filename in the *Enter AutoText Entries Here* box → click **Insert**. The phrase should appear in the correct place. You may need to alter the font style of the autotext to match the rest of the letter. You could also use the keyboard shortcut by typing in the three letter/digit code in the exam paper and pressing F3.

Copies and routing

You will be instructed to print two extra copies of this document and indicate the routing. Follow the instructions given for business letter layout in the Text Production notes (page 47).

EXERCISE WP 2.16

Recall the letterhead template stored as FELINE and key in the following document. Insert the autotext phrases as indicated. Use Comic Sans MS 12 font style for the letter but do not change the letterheading. Use a ragged right margin. Save as FELINE2 and print.

Our ref JM/SHL

Mrs S Hollings
48 Windsor Street
OADBY
LE9 4MP

Top + 2 copies please. One for Helen Martin and one for our files. Indicate routing.

Dear Mrs Hollings

Thank you for your letter asking about the facilities on offer at our boarding cattery. I note that you have two elderly cats that will need daily grooming.

We set up Feline Fancies over ten years ago. We can accommodate up to 50 cats at any one time. We live in the adjoining house so you can be sure that your pets are always in safe hands. Our business is open all year round and our reputation has grown mainly through word of mouth. Our superb facilities include

- modern accommodation blocks with plenty of room for the cats to exercise in their own run
- heated beds and underfloor heating in the runs during the winter months
- home pickup and drop-off service at no extra charge.

We also offer reduced rates for regular customers. If you decide to bring your cats to board with us, it is vital that you

Insert Autotext Phrase stored as REQ

We recommend that all potential customers visit our cattery before boarding their pets with us. To make an appointment, please contact me on the above number.

Insert Autotext Phrase stored as WEL

Yours sincerely

Judy McNabb
Proprietor

EXERCISE WP 2.17

Recall the letterhead template stored as ACCOUNT and key in the following document. Insert the autotext phrases as indicated. Use Tahoma 12 font style for the letter but do not change the letterheading. Use a ragged right margin. Save as ACCOUNT2 and print.

Our ref CH/1709/na

Top +2 please. One for Gabriel Gray and one for our files. Indicate routing.

Miss Olivia Osbourn
1400 Alabaster Avenue
ILFRACOMBE
Devon
EX34 6SS

Dear Miss Osbourn

I confirm that your application to open a current account with us has been approved. You will be receiving an introductory pack which should reach you within five working days. The pack will give you comprehensive information on how to run your account.

We list below some reasons why opening an account with us will be beneficial to you.

- You can access your account 24 hours a day.
- We can arrange for direct debits to be paid from your account.
- We have a wide range of accessible branches.

We are introducing new measures which are designed to combat fraud. Our staff may ask you to provide additional identification or will contact you to confirm instructions. We would ask you to be patient with these security measures. They are in place solely for your protection.

In the meantime, there are various steps that you can take to avoid becoming a victim of fraudulent practices.

Insert Autotext Phrase stored as PN2

Please be vigilant at all times and check your bank and card statements regularly. You should advise us immediately if you notice any unfamiliar transactions.

Insert Autotext Phrase stored as AM2

EXERCISE WP 2.18

Recall the letterhead template stored as FUND and key in the following document. Insert the autotext phrases as indicated. Use Tahoma 12 font style for the letter but do not change the letterheading. Use a ragged right margin. Save as FUND1 and print.

Our Ref NJ240

Insert Autotext Phrase stored as HU2

Further to our site meeting and very useful telephone call I am writing to confirm the points we agreed yesterday. I will arrange for the contractor to

Insert Autotext Phrase stored as CN2

Your company will

- deliver the greenhouse and take away all the packaging
- erect the greenhouse to the agreed specification and ensure that there is easy access for the electricity supply
- provide all the staging.

In return for your generous gift of the staging Pip North has agreed that this will be shown in the school publicity over the greenhouse. She is arranging for an official opening to take place and hopes that you will be able to attend.

We are very grateful for all your help and guidance. It is much appreciated both by us and the school and hopefully this greenhouse will prove a success with the children. As well as giving them enjoyment it will provide the school with a useful learning resource.

Our Partnership Fund supports 5 primary schools in the district. It is anticipated that within 2 years we can offer greenhouses to all the schools if this one is successful.

Yours sincerely

Top + 2 copies please. One for Pip North and one for our files. Indicate routing.

Jill Bacon
Fund Co-ordinator

AUDIO-TRANSCRIPTION LEVEL 2 PRACTICE EXERCISES

WITH DETAILED NOTES ON HOW TO WORK THE FOLLOWING DOCUMENTS:

- Letter
- Memo
- Advertisement
- Notice
- Report
- Article

LETTER

See the notes under Text Production (page 45) for detailed information on layout of business letters. Unless stated otherwise, the same rules apply to Audio-Transcription.

Candidate Information Sheet

The Candidate Information Sheet contains references, names, addresses and proper nouns. This is to help you with the spelling of such words.

Reference

Key in the reference exactly as shown on the reference sheet, with regard to spacing, punctuation and capitalisation. Do not add your initials to a reference, or add a *Your ref*, as this will incur a penalty.

Date

You must date this document with the date on which you work on it. See the detailed notes under Text Production (page 46).

Special mark

You will be instructed to insert a special mark in closed capitals.

Heading

Follow capitalisation and underlining as dictated.

Corrections to text

One of the words dictated in this document will be identified as an incorrect one, e.g. *We intend to order (Operator: correction) purchase a stock of ring binders*. In this case you would simply replace *order* with *purchase*.

Other than those dictated, you will not be tested on any other amendments to text.

Punctuation

All essential punctuation is dictated, except for the end of a paragraph when the word *paragraph* will indicate a final full stop followed by a clear linespace.

Enclosure(s)

You are required to indicate an enclosure(s) as indicated in the text. You must show clearly whether there are single or multiple enclosures. Follow the instructions given for business letter layout in the Text Production notes (page 47).

Copies and routing

You will be instructed to print two extra copies of this document and indicate the routing. Follow the instructions given for business letter layout in the Text Production notes (page 47).

Accessing audio exercises material

Candidate Information Sheets

Candidate Information Sheets follow for exercises:

- AT 2.1
- AT 2.2
- AT 2.3.

Templates

The letter template is available on the Hodder Plus website at **www.hodderplus.co.uk/ocrtextprocessing**. The same template can be used for all exercises.

Dictated documents

The dictation for the above exercises is available on the Hodder Plus website.

CANDIDATE INFORMATION SHEET AT 2.1

CANDIDATE INFORMATION SHEET

DOCUMENT 1

Included in dictation:

Progress
Sara Crowe
Geoff Randall
Managing Director
James Vine

References:

GR/RJ

Address:

18 Village Way
CROYDON
CR4 8AF

NB: All other instructions (eg courtesy titles, special mark, extra copies, headings etc) will be given in the dictation.

CANDIDATE INFORMATION SHEET AT 2.2

DOCUMENT 1

CANDIDATE INFORMATION SHEET

Included in dictation:

Amanda Hogan

Mary Farmer
Insurance Manager

James Roberts

Address:

91 Wessex Drive
GUILDFORD
Surrey
GU3 7JP

Reference(s):

MF/DP

NB: All other instructions (eg courtesy titles, headings etc) will be given in the dictation.

CANDIDATE INFORMATION SHEET AT 2.3

2

CANDIDATE INFORMATION SHEET

Included in dictation:

Mrs Helen King
Dalton Metcalfe
James Kelly

References:

DM/LD

Address:

27 Lime Avenue
NORWICH
NN1 8QJ

NB: All other instructions (eg courtesy titles, department names, headings etc) will be given in the dictation.

MEMO/ADVERTISEMENT/NOTICE

Layout and style

See the notes under Text Production (page 53) for detailed information on the layout of memo headings.

Reference

You must insert a reference in a memo. Key in the reference exactly as shown on the reference sheet, with regard to spacing, punctuation and capitalisation. Do not add your initials to a reference, or add a *Your ref*, as this will incur a penalty.

 You do not need to add a reference to an advertisement or notice.

Date

You must date a memo with the date on which you work on it. Acceptable styles are given in the Text Production notes for business letters (page 46).

 There is no need to date an advertisement or a notice.

Heading

You will be instructed to insert a heading. Follow capitalisation as dictated.

Punctuation

All essential punctuation is dictated, except for the end of a paragraph, when the word *paragraph* will indicate a final full stop followed by a clear linespace.

Emphasis

You will be instructed to emphasise a paragraph or sentence. Emboldening, closed capitals, underlining, centring or insetting are all acceptable. Ensure that you take the emphasis instruction off at the end of the relevant portion of text.

Centring

You will be instructed to centre one item of text in this document, e.g. a heading or a line of text.

Numbered paragraphs

When numbering paragraphs or items, you can key the numbers as you go along, using the tab key to align the following text, or you can use **Format →** **Bullets and Numbering →** select **Numbered**, and this will automatically add numbers and align the text.

Corrections to text

One of the words dictated in this document will be identified as an incorrect one, e.g. *The performance starts at 6 pm (Operator: correction) 1800 hours on Saturday.* In this case you would simply replace *6 pm* with *1800 hours*.

Other than those dictated, you will not be tested on any other amendments to text.

Accessing audio exercises material

Candidate Information Sheets

Candidate Information Sheets follow for exercises:

- AT 2.4
- AT 2.5
- AT 2.6
- AT 2.7
- AT 2.8
- AT 2.9
- AT 2.10
- AT 2.11
- AT 2.12.

Templates

The memo template is available on the Hodder Plus website at **www.hodderplus.co.uk/ocrtextprocessing**. The same template can be used for all exercises.

Dictated documents

The dictation for the above exercises is available on the Hodder Plus website.

CANDIDATE INFORMATION SHEET

DOCUMENT 2

Included in dictation:

Maria Delgado
Lucinda Parkinson

References:

LP/OD

Address:

NB: **All other instructions (eg courtesy titles, special mark, extra copies, headings etc) will be given in the dictation.**

CANDIDATE INFORMATION SHEET AT 2.5

DOCUMENT 2

CANDIDATE INFORMATION SHEET

Included in dictation:

Daniel Hobson

Charles Marshall

Address:

Reference(s):

DH/FW

NB: All other instructions (eg courtesy titles, headings etc) will be given in the dictation.

CANDIDATE INFORMATION SHEET AT 2.6

CANDIDATE INFORMATION SHEET

Included in dictation:

Anita Fernandez
Bradley Jenkins

References:

BJ/GA

Address:

NB: All other instructions (eg courtesy titles, department names, headings etc) will
        be given in the dictation.

CANDIDATE INFORMATION SHEET AT 2.7

CANDIDATE INFORMATION SHEET

DOCUMENT 2

Included in dictation:

Progress

References:

Address:

NB: All other instructions (eg courtesy titles, special mark, extra copies, headings etc) will be given in the dictation.

CANDIDATE INFORMATION SHEET AT 2.8

DOCUMENT 2

CANDIDATE INFORMATION SHEET

Included in dictation:

Helen Dawson

Address:

Reference(s):

NB: All other instructions (eg courtesy titles, headings etc) will be given in the dictation.

CANDIDATE INFORMATION SHEET AT 2.9

CANDIDATE INFORMATION SHEET

Included in dictation:

Chester
Human Resources Department

References:

Address:

NB: All other instructions (eg courtesy titles, department names, headings etc) will be given in the dictation.

CANDIDATE INFORMATION SHEET AT 2.10

CANDIDATE INFORMATION SHEET

DOCUMENT 2

Included in dictation:

Progress College
Westwood Way

References:

Address:

NB: All other instructions (eg courtesy titles, special mark, extra copies, headings etc) will be given in the dictation.

DOCUMENT 2

CANDIDATE INFORMATION SHEET

Included in dictation:

Swindon

Address:

References:

NB: All other instructions (eg courtesy titles, headings etc) will be given in the dictation.

CANDIDATE INFORMATION SHEET AT 2.12

2

CANDIDATE INFORMATION SHEET

Included in dictation:

Argentine

References:

Address:

NB: All other instructions (eg courtesy titles, department names, headings etc) will be given in the dictation.

REPORT/ARTICLE

Heading

You will be instructed to insert a heading. Follow capitalisation as dictated.

Punctuation

All essential punctuation is dictated, except for the end of a paragraph, when the word *paragraph* will indicate a final full stop followed by a clear linespace.

Linespacing

You will be instructed to change the linespacing of a section of text. At the beginning of the section you will hear *Operator: please change to … linespacing for the following paragraph.* At the end of that section you will be told *Operator: that is the end of the paragraph in … linespacing.* Immediately you hear that instruction, return to the original linespacing for the rest of the document.

Leave at least one clear linespace before and after the table, consistently.

Corrections to text

One of the words dictated in this document will be identified as an incorrect one, e.g. *The agenda (Operator: correction) minutes are available for inspection.* In this case you would simply replace *agenda* with *minutes.* Other than those dictated, you will not be tested on any other amendments to text.

Allocation of vertical space

You will be instructed to leave a vertical space within the document. The simplest method is to use **Enter** to create sufficient linespaces. In *Print Layout View* the ruler line to the left of the screen will allow you to work out the spacing.

Distraction element

For the purpose of these exercises, a sheet headed 'Instructions for Invigilator' is provided in this section. It contains extra text for document 3. During the dictation for document 3 you will hear *Operator: this information was given to you earlier.* This is your prompt to add the words at this point.

However, in a live exam, about 15–20 minutes after the start of the examination the invigilator will announce this short sentence, which includes several words to be added to document 3. You will need to write this down so that you can add it at the appropriate point in document 3.

Table

This document contains a table of three or four columns. The information will be dictated in logical order, with one pause before a single figure, e.g. *Hodder Textbooks – TP2 – (Operator: one moment please) six thousand.* Each line should be keyed in horizontally, using the tab key to move between columns, ensuring that data in columns and column headings are aligned consistently. Leave a clear linespace after the headings. Work in *Page Layout View.*

   Column widths are dictated for those candidates who wish to key the table using preset tabs. The following notes apply to those using the table function.

Displaying tabular work using tables function

- Column widths can be altered by dragging the column borders with the mouse.
- Extra linespaces can be created by pressing **Enter** from within the cell. Avoid leaving empty cells.
- Leave a clear linespace after the headings.
- Leave equal linespacing before and after the table.
- Gridlines are useful while keying in, but are not required in the printout. To stop the gridlines from printing, first select the table then use **Format** → **Borders and Shading** → **Borders** → select **None**.

Accessing audio exercises material

Candidate Information Sheets and Instructions for Invigilator

Candidate Information Sheets and Instructions for Invigilator follow for exercises:

- AT 2.13
- AT 2.14
- AT 2.15.

Dictated documents

The dictation for the above exercises is available on the Hodder Plus website at **www.hodderplus.co.uk/ocrtextprocessing**.

CANDIDATE INFORMATION SHEET AT 2.13

2

CANDIDATE INFORMATION SHEET

DOCUMENT 3

Included in dictation:

References:

Address:

NB: All other instructions (eg courtesy titles, special mark, extra copies,
headings etc) will be given in the dictation.

DOCUMENT 3

INSTRUCTIONS TO INVIGILATOR:

About 15-30 minutes after the start of the examination, announce that for

Document 3:

it could make your home more attractive for sale or rent.

CANDIDATE INFORMATION SHEET AT 2.14

CANDIDATE INFORMATION SHEET

Included in dictation:

Mayfields Country Estate
Sir Willoughby Duncan-Smythe

References:

Address:

NB: All other instructions (eg courtesy titles, department names, headings etc) will be given in the dictation.

INSTRUCTIONS FOR INVIGILATOR

About 15-30 minutes after the start of the examination, announce that for Document 3
The preliminary inspection of the cottage and barn at Mayfields Country Estate

CANDIDATE INFORMATION SHEET AT 2.15

DOCUMENT 3

CANDIDATE INFORMATION SHEET

Included in dictation:

Progress Coach Tours

Norfolk
Dover Harbour
Brighton
London
Channel Islands

Address:

Reference(s):

NB: All other instructions (eg courtesy titles, headings etc) will be given in the dictation.

INSTRUCTIONS FOR INVIGILATOR

DOCUMENT 3

About 15 – 30 minutes after the start of the examination, announce that for Document 3:

With all holidays costing more than four hundred pounds this service is free.

EXAM WORK

4

This section provides hints for exam work, together with three new practice exams for each unit, similar to the OCR standard. The hints and complete exams for each different unit are grouped together.

Hints pages

Hints pages precede each set of exams. They remind you of the skills you will have acquired in the practice exercises and of the methods you can use to successfully complete each exam. Take the time to read the hints relating to each unit before attempting the exam in that subject. You can refer to the hints as you work through each practice exam. *Of course, you may not refer to the notes or hints in this book at the time of sitting the real live exams.*

Practice exams

There are three new complete practice exams for each unit. Recall text for these exams is available on the Hodder Plus website (see below). Once you have finished a complete exam, proofread it and correct any errors. Make sure you have saved the final version of each document, using the filenames indicated, and print copies. Find the correct worked example of the exam in Chapter 5 and proofread your copy against this. If you are a member of a group, you may find it helpful to proofread each other's work, or your tutor may wish to take in your work for marking.

Recall text from the Hodder Plus website

You will need to access files on the Hodder Plus website at **www.hodder-plus.co.uk/ocrtextprocessing** in order to carry out the following:

• insert files for letter, memo, press release and file note headings
• recall text to insert into your files
• access dictation for the audio-transcription exams.

The templates that you will need to recall for Text Production and Audio-Transcription are saved under the following filenames:

LETTERHEAD	MEMO
FILE_NOTE	PRESS_RELEASE

For the purpose of these practice exams, you may use the same letterhead for any of the Text Production or Audio-Transcription documents, although some of the worked examples may show different letterheads. The same applies to other templates, where slight variations may occur.

The letterhead templates with autotext and the recall text for Word Processing are saved under the filenames given in each document in the practice exams.

Audio-Transcription

The Candidate Information Sheets (containing proper nouns) and Instruction to Invigilator Sheets (with information for document 3) are provided in this section. Dictated material is saved under the filenames given to each document and accessed from the Hodder Plus website at **www.hodderplus.co.uk/ ocrtextprocessing**.

TEXT PRODUCTION LEVEL 2 PRACTICE EXAMS

WITH HINTS SHEETS COVERING

- Skills checklist
- General hints
- Hints for each document

HINTS FOR EXAM WORK: OCR TEXT PRODUCTION LEVEL 2

Checklist of skills

You need to be able to carry out the following before you attempt the practice exams:

- recall letterhead, memo/press release/file note headings into your files
- lay out a letter
- complete memo/press release/file note headings
- alter linespacing
- emphasise and underline text and headings
- insert and delete text
- create new paragraphs, insert and close up spaces
- interpret and carry out amendment and correction signs
- expand abbreviations from OCR list
- spell words from OCR list of business vocabulary
- correct identified grammatical and apostrophe errors
- correct non-identified typographical, spelling and punctuation errors
- incorporate information from another document

- indicate enclosure(s)
- add automatic page numbering.

General

- Start a **New** file for each document.
- Use either the **Header** or **Footer** facility to record your name, centre number and document number (together with automatic page numbering on any multi-paged document) on each printout.
- Use **Insert** to recall a letterhead or memo/press release/file note template into your own new file, then use **Save As** to give it a file name. The templates are available on the Hodder Plus website at **www.hodderplus.co.uk/ ocrtextprocessing**.
- Thereafter click on the **Save** screen icon frequently, as you work.
- As a general rule for these exam units, carry out editing instructions as you key in, apart from linespacing instructions, which can be left to the end.
- As you complete each instruction, tick it off on the question paper. This makes it easier to keep track, particularly when working on a multi-paged document.
- As you key in an email or internet address, your computer changes the text colour to blue and underscores it. It can be left like this but, if you wish, you may alter it by marking it then selecting **Format** → **Font** → **Underline** (none) → **Colour** (black).
- You may print as often as you wish, both during and immediately after the exam time allocation. However, remember that the process is time-consuming, particularly when many candidates are involved, so you should proofread carefully from the screen prior to printing.
- Proofread a second time from the hard copy.
- **Ensure you have SAVED your final edited version of each document before you log off at the end of the session.**

Document 1: letter

- This document must be printed on the OCR letterhead template.
- It must be dated with the date on which you are doing the practice exam.
- Key in any references exactly as shown. Only insert a *Your reference* if one is given. Do not add your own initials.
- Key the special mark immediately before the name and address.
- Key in text, making amendments according to the draft.
- Follow draft for capitalisation.
- Spelling and punctuation errors must be identified by you and corrected.
- Correct circled grammar and apostrophe errors.
- Abbreviations, which are not circled, should be identified by you and expanded. (Some abbreviations should *not* be expanded – these are listed in

the Unit Specification)
- Use a calendar or diary to check the date for the postdating item. Only the day and month are essential. It is not necessary to include the year.
- When underlining text, ensure that the line does not overshoot either end of the relevant text. It may include any punctuation that is part of the final word.
- Do not number single-page documents, but continuation sheets must be numbered. Use **Insert → Page Numbers** to customise your numbering.
- Remember to indicate any enclosure(s) mentioned in the body of the letter.
- Proofread carefully, using the **Spellcheck**, and check that you have not omitted or misplaced text.

Document 2: memo/press release/file note
- These documents must be printed on the relevant OCR template.
- These documents must be dated with the date on which you are doing the practice exam.
- Key in text, making amendments according to the draft.
- Spelling and punctuation errors must be identified by you and corrected.
- Correct circled grammar and apostrophe errors.
- Abbreviations, which are not circled, should be identified by you and expanded.
- There may be an enclosure(s) indicated in the memo, but not the file note or press release.

Document 3: report or article
- Key in text, making amendments according to the draft. You may leave linespacing alterations to the end.
- Follow draft for capitalisation.
- Typographical and spelling errors must be identified and corrected by you.
- Abbreviations, which are not circled, should be identified by you and expanded.
- Grammatical errors are circled and must be corrected.
- When altering the linespacing of paragraphs of text, ensure that the linespacing between the paragraphs and before and after that section is consistent.
- When emphasising a portion of text, ensure that only the indicated portion is emphasised. This is usually carried out by emboldening or using closed capitals.
- If the document runs to more than a single page, the continuation sheet must be numbered. Use **Insert → Page Numbers** to customise your numbering. Single sheets should not be numbered.
- In a live exam, a separate sheet of extra text will be handed to you by the

invigilator 15–20 minutes after the start of the exam. This is for insertion into document 3. Tuck your copy into the question paper at the relevant point, so that you don't forget to include it, otherwise you will be penalised 1 mark for each omitted word. *In these practice exams, the sheet of extra text is included with the draft document.*

- Proofread carefully, using the **Spellcheck**, and check that you have not omitted or misplaced text.

EXAM TP 2.A

Our ref BA/cn

Mrs D Richardson
56 Waterford Rd
WELLING
Kent
DA16 2JB

Mark this
BY HAND

Dear Mrs Richardson

Thank you for your ~~last~~ ~~recent~~ order for a new ✓
greenhouse. We will be able to deliver this on
Tuesday (give date for second Tuesday of next month)
and your greenhouse will be built the same
day. We will need to lay the concrete base
at least five (day) before delivery. It is
necy to ensure that the concrete has
had suficient time to dry before building
your greenhouse. Please contact my sec
in order to arrange a day and time to
lay the base

We (has) much pleasure in enclosing our
latest cat giving details and prices of
our greenhouse accessories. As you can see
we sell a wide range of ~~heaters, vents~~
~~staging and other~~ accessories in many (size's)
and colours. If you would like to order
any of these items please let us know
asap and we may be able to deliver them
at the same time as your greenhouse.
                    and other garden buildings
All our greenhouses∧come with a guarantee
and we will send this to you at the end
of next month. [We hope that you will
enjoy growing plants in your new greenhouse.
If you have any questions then please
do not hesitate to contact us again.

Yrs sncly

Belinda Alison
Sales Manager

typist/operator: this is a press release

Company Name   Progress Builders
Contact Person   James Doyle

Progress Builders is pleased to offer a discount on any work undertaken within the next three months.

This is a good opp to get all those outstanding project's completed. We can give estimates immed.

discounts will be given on all types of building work. However large or small the job (we can do the work/we know) to a very high standard.

All our workers are ▼ experiensed builders. As a result we are able to carry out loft conversions as well as building extensions.

If you would like any further information or an estimate please contact us.

experts in their field and are

typist/operator: an extra paragraph for this document will be handed to you by the invigilator during the course of the examination

double linespacing except where indicated

OFFICE MOVE

This report is to be ~~sent~~ circulated to all department heads who will then circulate to their ✓ staff.

Everyone has to be aware of what needs to be done.

The lease on our current office space runs out at the end of next month. The directors have been looking at other premises in town. Last week a lease was signed on new office space. *These new premises are in the High St and will provide us with more space than we have currently.*

Clearing of the Rubbish and Packing Boxes

Next Fri there will be a rubbish collection. Staff must label items for disposal and these should include any broken electrical equipment, desks and chairs.

emphasise this sentence

It should be noted that all documents must be shredded before being put into the paper recycling sacks. Further supplies of these sacks have been bought.

Old data disks must be placed in the boxes supplied. *These will be given to a specialist co. All data on the disks will be wiped and then the disks will be destroyed.*

, and will be available soon

(these paragraphs only in single linespacing)

All department heads will be attending a mtg to discuss the best layout for the new offices. When this has been done the layout will be made available to all members of staff.

It will be necessary for staff to spend at least two hour each week helping to pack items into boxes. A rota will be arranged for this purpose. It may be that we will have to spend more or less time on packing. We can assess this again soon.

Please let your manager know if you are willling to work over time in order to help with the packing.

(typist/operator: insert extra paragraph here)

The directors is sure that the new offices will enable us to expand our busines and extra space will allow us to diversify and employ more staff.

Prospects for the Future

In order to keep the disruption to the office to a minimum that the office continues to run smoothly the move will take place over the course of a week. This means that only one departmnt at any time will be disrupted.

We are looking forward to the move and we know that our stafff will do what they can to help make this a huge success.

typist/operator: this is the extra paragraph for the report

The week before the move the removal men will issue us with numbered labels. These

labels should be put on chiars, desks and cabinets. The numbers will corrispond with

the new office plan. The removal men will therfore be able to place all it5ems in the

correct rooms.

EXAM TP 2.B

Our ref   JF/EN43

Mr Martin Reid
Technotrial Limited
64 Humberstone Road
BIRMINGHAM
B2 6XJ

(Mark this
PRIVATE AND CONFIDENTIAL)

Dr Martin

Thank you for your letter enquiring about the benefits of adopting a car share scheme for your employees. I am pleased to hear that you are thinking of reviewing your co's business mileage.

throughout the United Kingdom

Car share schemes are becoming very popular/. Many people (believes) that it is a greener alternative to owning a car. It is also less expensive. Some schemes, like ours, require clients to settle their account monthly. You pay only for your mileage, plus a daily or hourly rental fee. [In Birmingham we have a network of dedicated car share spaces. We gntee that there will be an available vehicle within 10 (minute's) walk of your office. There are approx 150 parking (space) devoted to our cars. Reserve your car online or by telephone

If you would like to discus the ~~issue~~ matter further, please ✓ telephone to arrange an appointment. In the meantime, I enclose our latest info sheet. We are currently offering new business clients a 20% discount if they register before Friday (give date for last Friday of next month).

I hope that you will use Progress Cars as your car share provider. I look forward to hearing from you ~~in the very near future~~.

Yrs sincerely

Jason Fullhurst
Marketing Executive

typist/operator: this is a file note

From   Tanya Brown
Position   Evening Supervisor
File Number   49632

Yesterday Mr James Ecclestone telephoned. His customer ref is E19842. He would like his wife to be added to his membership. Her name is Andrea. she is an expereinced driver and holds a clean British driving licence.

Unfortunately when he called the client database was being tested. I did not have an opp to update his records. Mr Ecclestones' details need to be amended urgently as his wife wishes to use a Progress car next week.

I have requested a smart card in her name. Mrs Ecclestone will call in to collect it at the office.

and it will be ready later today

Typist/operator: an extra paragraph for this document will be handed to you by the invigilator during the course of the examination

double linespacing except where indicated

CAR SHARING WITH PROGRESS CARS

Over recent years Progress Cars has been developing its car sharing scheme across the United Kingdom. With dedicated car spaces in mo@re than ten cities, Progress now has more than 5000 clients. Read on to see how you could benefit from becoming a member of our club.

THE PRICE OF SHARING

Car sharing not only makes financial sense, it also help the environment.

For every car shared, it is ~~estimated~~ thought that six cars are taken off the road. Sharing a car means that you pay only when you need to make a journey. Costs such as road tax, insurance, repairs and depreciation are no longer an issue.

WHY SHARE?

It costs just £50 for an individaul to join the club. Companies can register for £150 and this covers the subscription for up to ten members of staff. Membership is renewed annually. In addittion, members pay a daily or hourly rate for the use of the vehicle. A 1.4 litre diesel hatchback costs £4 per hour or £40 for each 24-hour period. Larger vehicles and vans cost slightly more. For each day of the booking, you get 30 mile of free petrol. After that, mileage plus petrol is charged at 25p per mile.

These paragraphs only in single linespacing

HOW THE SCHEME WORKS

Whenever you wish to book a car, let us know by tel or email. Tell us the length of the booking and your preferred pick-up location. We will confirm by text message or email. We will indicate the make, colour and registration number of the car.

At the colllection point, use your Progress smartcard to unlock the vehicle. Once inside, use the card to acess the keys from the glove compartment. Enter your pin number onto the keypad on the dash board and drive away.

On your return please leave the car in its designated space. Your a/c is payable at the end of the month.

BUSNESS CLIENTS

typist/operator: insert extra paragraph here

type of vehicle required, the

JOIN US NOW

To join our club, visit our website: www.progresscars.co.uk. Complete the online form with the necy details. That is all it takes. look forward to welcoming you to our club soon! We will be in contact with details of how to proceed

typist/operator: this is the extra paragraph for the article

Emphasise this sentence

Progress Cars offers business clients all the advantages of operating a fleet of cars, but without the fixed costs and depreciation. If you use our cars on a daily basis, we can even locate our vehicles in your own office car park. For most orgs car sharing clubs work out cheaper than paying staff to use their own vehicle for business travel.

EXAM TP 2.C

Our ref   PB/MA

Ms Lucy Chaston
89 Wilmslow Cres
BRACKEN ASH
Norfolk
NR14 6YA

Mark this CONFIDENTIAL

Dr Lucy

As you know, our co is undergoing a period of major reorganisation. The aim (are) to streamline our operations in order to improve our efficiency. As a result, all staff are being asked to reapply for their jobs The attached doc outlines the posts in your section for which you can apply. Please tick 3 (box) indicating your preferred choice. [The application process is in 2 (part's). Firstly, all employees are obliged to attend an assessment day. The date for this is shown on the enclosed info sheet. Secondly, a week or so later, interviews will be held. Your interview date is Thursday (give date for second Thursday of next month) at 9.30 am at head office. You should allow at least 2 hours for this.

We appreciate that this is an worrying anxious time for all staff. (✓) However, we do not expect any redundancies. Those employees nearing retirement will be offered a very tempting finansial package. Other staff will be given jobs based on their performance on the assessment day and at interview. This whole process should be achieved within 3 months.

Our Chief Executive wishes to thank you all for your loyal commitment over many years and looks forward to working with you in the future.

Yours sncly

Paul Bulmer
Director of Human Resources

typist/operator: this is a memorandum

To   Frances Westwell

From Fadil Mehta

Ref   FM/DAC

Our org▼ is concerned at the current skills shortage in the field of horticulture.

With this in mind, we have agreed to man a stand at the local Careers Fair. this is to be held in the autumn. It would give us an opp to highlight the many career (paths') (open to people of all ages (in horticulture).

With your years of experience in this subject, I should be grateful if you would write a short article on A5 paper for this event. Please let me see a draft copy before the end of next week.

, in common with other research institutes,

typist/operator: extra paragraphs for this document will be handed to you by the invigilator during the course of the examination

double linespacing except where indicated

A CAREER IN HORTICULTURE

Horticulture is defined as the art or sceince of growing garden plants. A career in this field can be varied and fulfilling. This ~~vast~~ *huge* industry is one of the largest ✓ employers in the British Isles, with jobs ranging from planting seeeds to landscape design. Many of these involve working in the open air. Other opnings are in garden centres where numerous opportunities are available for both skilled and unskilled workers.

GREENKEEPER

insert extra paragraphs here

PARK RANGER

The duties of a park ranger are diverse. The main aims are to protect the park resources for the future and to look after its visitors. Some rangers provide a useful information service. This may include weather forecasts or the siting of a rare plant or bird. In addition, they might lead guided tours, *deal with forest fires,* rescue animals, etc. *Education to degree level in a relevant subject is necy. A good knowledge of trees and plants is recomended.*

GARDEN DESIGN

If you enjoy sport and like outdoor life, then emp as a greenkeeper would be a healthy and satisfying career for you. Golf greenkeepers aim to provide the best playing

these paragraphs only in single linespacing

conditions for club members and matches.

Training can be undertaken in the work place. Assessment is carried out on the job and can lead to a National Vocational Qualification. On the other hand, a National Certificate can be achieved by attending a college course. This may be studied full or part time for one or two year.

GARDEN CENTRE CAREERS

Garden centres provide good career paths in many misc jobs. ~~Plant retail outlets are currently increasing all over the country.~~ These include marketing, sales and management. For a junior post, a knowledge of plants is vital. A horticultural qualification is also helpful. Senior posts would require a degree in an appropriate subject, as well as experience in the chosen option.

Other options are in forestry, growing and developping seeds, floral work and research. Refs to these and other careers in this industry can be found on the Internet.

typist/operator: these are the extra paragraphs for the article

A career in garden design can be very rewarding. Students come from all
walks of life and do not need experience in graphic art. All sizes of garden
have to be planned and drawn to scale. Family gardens will include children's
play areas and space for relaxation. If the garden are large enough, water
features and fruit and vegtable plots may be built in.

Dipl;oma courses are open to students of all ages and with no formal training.

A passsion for gardens is a key factor for a successful career in this field.

emphasise this sentence

WORD PROCESSING LEVEL 2 PRACTICE EXAMS

WITH HINTS SHEETS COVERING

- Skills checklist
- General hints
- Hints for each document

HINTS FOR EXAM WORK: OCR WORD PROCESSING LEVEL 2

Checklist of skills

You need to be able to carry out the following before you attempt the practice exams:

- recall a letterhead and documents
- add automatic page numbering for pages 2 and onwards, but not page 1
- delete and insert page breaks
- add headers and footers
- alter margins to adjust line length
- inset, justify and centre text
- alter linespacing and leave vertical spacing
- alter font style and size
- format a document for landscape printing
- emphasise and underscore text
- interpret amendment and correction signs
- select and insert autotext phrases
- change specified words automatically by using find and replace facility
- move and copy text by using cut/copy and paste facility
- insert and resize a picture
- present information in tables format
- number items automatically
- produce extra copies and indicate routing
- sort lists in alphabetical, numerical and chronological order
- carry out an automatic word count.

General

- Start a **New** file for each document.
- Use either the **Header** or **Footer** facility to record your name, centre number and document number (together with automatic page numbering on a multi-paged document) on each printout.

- Recall text for these exams is available on the Hodder Plus website at **www.hodderplus.co.uk/ocrtextprocessing**. Use **Insert** and select the name indicated in the document instructions. Use **Save As** to give it the file name indicated.
- Thereafter click on the **Save** icon frequently, as you work.
- As a general rule, for these exam units, key in the extra text first and then carry out editing instructions. Leave any linespacing and vertical spacing editing to the end.
- As you complete each instruction tick it off on the question paper. This makes it easier to keep track, particularly when working on a multi-paged document.
- As you key in an email or internet address, your computer changes the text colour to blue and underscores it. It can be left like this but, if you wish, you may alter it by marking it then selecting **Format** → **Font** → **Underline** (none) → **Colour** (black).
- You may print as often as you wish, both during and immediately after the exam time allocation. However, remember that the process is time-consuming, particularly when many candidates are involved, so you should proofread carefully from the screen prior to printing.
- Proofread a second time from the hard copy.
- **Ensure you have SAVED your final edited version of each document before you log off at the end of the session.**

Document 1: article/information sheet/report

- Recall the stored document as instructed.
- Key in handwritten text first then carry out editing instructions, ticking them off as you complete them.
- To adjust the top and left margins use **File** → **Page Setup** or drag the margins on the ruler (you need to be in *Page Layout View*). *NB: A4 paper is 21 cm wide.*
- This is a multi-paged document and the pages should be numbered as instructed, omitting the page number from page 1. Use **Insert** → **Page Numbers** to fully customise your numbering. Remember to put the page number in the footer if you already have a header and vice versa.
- To insert a **Header** or **Footer** use **View** → **Header and Footer** → select either one → key specified text in box using text alignment icons to place it correctly.
- To **Move** or **Copy** text, carry out the following:
  - when you **Move** a section of text it should appear *once* in the document
  - use the **Cut** and **Paste** icons
  - when you **Copy** a section of text it should appear *twice* in the document
  - use the **Copy** and **Paste** icons.
- To change recurring words in the document use **Edit** → **Replace** and enter the word to be found, then the replacement word. Select **Replace All**.

- Leave linespacing, vertical spacing alterations and page breaks to the end. The simplest way to create a page break is to hold down **Control** and press the **Enter** key. This instruction can be undone by using the **Show/Hide** icon (¶) to reveal the page break instruction, highlighting *page break* and deleting it.
- Proofread carefully, using the **Spellcheck**, and check that you have not omitted or misplaced text.

Document 2: notice/poster/advertisement for display

- Recall the stored document as instructed.
- Key in handwritten text first, then carry out editing instructions.
- You are asked to change the *size* of font of one portion of text. You should not alter the *style* of font.
- Insert a stored picture where indicated, using the given filename to recall it. To change its measurements, you can drag the width arrows, but, for accuracy:
    - right click mouse → **Format Picture** → **Size** → change measurement
    - to allow for word wrapping, select **Format Picture** → **Layout** → select text wrapped to left or right of picture as indicated in draft.
- To sort a list use **Table** → **Sort** → **Ascending/Descending**.
- Leave the word count until the very end. Save the document, then use **Tools** → **Word Count** and key the number of words specified at the bottom of the document. Save again.
- Print a copy of the document in landscape, using **FILE** → **PAGE SETUP** → **PAPER SIZE** → select **ORIENTATION** (Landscape).
- Proofread carefully, checking that you have carried out all the amendments and have not omitted any text.

Document 3: table

- Recall the stored document as instructed.
- Use the tables function for tabular work to allow you to carry out the editing efficiently.

Displaying tabular work using tables function

- Work in *Print Layout View*.
- To insert a table use **Table** → **Insert** → **Table** → select **Columns** and **2 Rows**. Create more rows as required by positioning your cursor in the last column and pressing the tab key.
- Key each line horizontally, and use the tab key or cursors to move between cells.
- Follow draft for capitalisation.

- Decimal points in money and measurements must be aligned.
- **Save** your work as soon as you have keyed in all the text. If some of your work is lost when editing the table, you should be able to recall the document at the point that you last saved it.
- Proofread your keyed text before moving or modifying the text, as it is easier to check it against the draft at that stage.
- Column widths can easily be altered by dragging the borders using your mouse.
- Extra line spaces can be inserted by pressing **Enter** from within the cell.
- Use **Table** → **Sort** → **Ascending/Descending** to sort columns numerically or alphabetically.
- Use **Table** → **Select Row** or **Select Column** in order to mark text to be moved, then use the **Cut** and **Paste** icons to move it.
- Use **Table** → **Merge Cells** to place headings over more than one column. This should be left to the end, as it can interfere with selecting and moving text.
- To get rid of grid lines use **Format** → **Borders and Shading** → select **None**.
- Proofread again, checking that headings and columns are aligned consistently, and each modification and editing instruction has been completed. Make sure you have included the text before and after the table.

Document 4: letter

- Recall the letterhead template as instructed. The autotext phrases you need for this document are set up within the letterhead template.
- Use the font style and size instructed throughout the document, but do not change the letterhead.
- The letter must be dated with the date on which you are doing the practice exam.
- Key in any references exactly as shown. Only insert a *Your ref* if one is given. Do not add your own initials.
- To recall and insert an autotext phrase, move your cursor to the insert point then use **Insert** → **Autotext** → key the stored filename in the *Enter Autotext Entries Here* box → click **Insert**. The autotext should appear in the correct place. You may need to alter the font style of the autotext to match the rest of the letter. You could also use the keyboard shortcut by typing in the three letter/digit code in the exam paper and pressing F3.
- To route extra copies, key the routing information on the document and print three copies. Tick in pen against the name on one copy, and against *File* on the other copy. Routing may also be shown by using a symbol, e.g. √, → or by emboldening, underscoring or highlighting. Pencil marks are not acceptable.
- Proofread carefully, using the **Spellcheck**, and check that you have not omitted or misplaced text.

EXAM WP 2.A

Recall the article stored as EXERCISE. Amend as shown. Change to double linespacing (except where indicated). Adjust the left margin to 6 cm and the top margin to 7cm. Use full justification. Save as EX2 and print one copy.

FITNESS

With today's sedentary lifestyle, regular exercise ~~is essential to keep fit~~ should become part of your daily routine. Young and old alike can follow a fitness regime. The guidelines for an adult suggest 30 minutes per day but this can be split into 3 sessions, each of 10 minutes. Some people will find this much easier to sustain. Exercise does not have to take place in a gym. Walking to the shops, for example, will count as part of your fitness regime. Try getting off the bus one stop before you normally do and walk that extra distance to your home.

You should always use the stairs instead of a lift or escalator. Put this into practice whilst shopping, at railway stations or in multi-storey car parks.

Page 2 starts here

(Z)

Exercise ~~can be enjoyable and beneficial~~ is an important part of a healthy life. It improves fitness and mental awareness. It is a contributory factor in maintaining a healthy weight whilst avoiding the dangers of obesity. (A)

Combine moderate exercise with more energetic activities to create a proper balance. Take up new leisure interests that involve exertion of some kind.

This section only in single linespacing

Once regular exercise has been introduced into your daily routine, it is essential to stay motivated. Keep reminding yourself of the reasons for starting your fitness regime. Chemicals and hormones released in the brain during exercise help to reduce stress levels. On a cold, wet day when you would rather not go out for a brisk walk, remind yourself of how much better you will feel afterwards.

Page 3 starts here

(✓)

Set yourself ~~attainable goals~~ achievable objectives. This will convince you that you are making steady progress towards your ultimate goal.

These could include gardening, swimming, cycling and home decorating.

Number the pages ensuring that Page 1 is not numbered

The time spent exercising is never wasted.

Use the quality time to escape problems or worries ~~in your everyday life~~ whilst improving your fitness and wellbeing.

Inset this section 4.5 cm from left margin

Exercise is especially good for elderly people. It is important that they should retain their mobility as much as possible.

Walking and gardening are two activities that will improve co-ordination and balance whilst strengthening muscles.

Move to point marked Z

Some cycle paths also provide interesting and varied places to walk. If you are near a canal, walk along the bank. You will benefit from the exercise and can see all kinds of wildlife at the same time.

Copy this sentence to point marked A

Remember that by adopting a healthy lifestyle, you can set an example to your children or grandchildren. Children often go to school by car and have very little daily physical activity outside playtime at school. Young people need at least 60 minutes of moderate exertion each day. A high proportion of this time should be devoted to exercise that strengthens bones and muscles and increases flexibility.

Change regime to programme throughout this document

Insert WELLBEING to appear as a header at the right margin on every page

Recall the advertisement stored as CLUB. Amend as shown. Save as CLUB2. Print a copy in landscape on one sheet of A4 paper.

OPEN DAY

PROGRESS FITNESS CLUB

and tone up flabby muscles

Do you want a healthier lifestyle? Do you need to lose weight/? Do you want to improve your general wellbeing?

Let us help you to achieve these goals. Start to change your life for the better.

Come along and see what our club can offer. ← This sentence only in a larger font size

Gym
Cycling
Cross country running
Swimming
Water sports
Walking
Weight training

Sort into exact alphabetical order

Centre this section only

Experienced trainers are on hand to give advice and guidance on the best programme for you. Meet like-minded people who want to improve their fitness.

Start with an easy programme. Gently increase to more strenuous exertion. Once you have had the chance to try some of the activities, we hope you will decide to become a member of our club.

We have a limited number of vacancies. We are looking for enthusiastic members who will take advantage of all our facilities.

Insert here the picture stored as GYM. Change measurement to 4.5 cm wide with the text wrapped to the right of the picture.

Contact our secretary on 01809 681481 in the first instance for full details.

On completion ensure you have saved your work and then use your software facilities to perform a word count. Key in this figure on a separate line below the final line of text.

Recall the document stored as BOUQUET. Retain the Arial 11 font throughout the document. Save as BOUQUET2 and print one copy.

PROGRESS BOUQUETS

We have recently introduced a new online service that supplies quality goods and a range of special offers at affordable prices. We pride ourselves on providing the best value for money.

Leave a vertical space of at least 7cm here

DESCRIPTION	OFFER	DETAILS FOR ORDERING	
		ITEM NUMBER	SPECIAL PRICE £
BUDGET SELECTION OF FLOWERS AND PLANTS			
Hand-tied button chrysanthemums	Textured sleeve	BFP22	15.99
Fragrant climbing jasmine	Terracotta pot	BFP36	14.99
Mixed single carnations	Free postage	BFP21	9.99
Elegant purple orchid	Ceramic pot	BFP24	16.99
Fuchsia spray carnations	Plain vase	BFP35	11.99
SPECIAL OCCASIONS AND DIAMOND COLLECTION			
Oriental lilies with roses	Free wine	SDC45	39.99
Gerbera and chrysanthemums	Luxury wrap	SDC47	32.95
Fragrant lilac, freesia and roses	Glass vase	SDC42	27.75
Mixed carnations with statice	Liqueur truffles	SDC49	25.00
Luxury cream roses	Crystal bowl	SDC54	29.99

We have been established for over 20 years. We cater for all occasions. We guarantee that our flowers will remain fresh for at least 10 days.

Please sort SPECIAL PRICE £ column into exact numerical order within each section starting with the highest figure. Ensure all corresponding details are also rearranged.

Modify layout so that SPECIAL OCCASIONS AND DIAMOND COLLECTION section comes before BUDGET SELECTION OF FLOWERS AND PLANTS section

Recall the letterhead template stored as DEALS and key in the following document. Insert the autotext phrases as indicated. Use Comic Sans MS 12 font style for the letter but do not change the letterheading. Use full justification. Save as DEALS2 and print.

Our ref CP/VS/CC

Insert Autotext Phrase stored as AD2

Thank you for your letter. I confirm that your request to convert your token points to vouchers is receiving our attention. These vouchers can be exchanged for goods or services at any of the participating businesses listed in our brochure.

Some popular choices are given below.
- Book a holiday or short break from the wide selection on offer.
- Treat yourself to a night at the theatre and one night's luxury accommodation.
- Choose from a range of leisure activities or club membership deals.

Visit our website at www.progressdeals.co.uk for full details of the terms and conditions relating to the implementation of this voucher scheme.

Please be aware that certain conditions apply when exchanging vouchers.

Insert Autotext Phrase stored as TS2

Our vouchers are only valid for a period of six months. Regrettably, there is no facility to renew them so you should ensure that they are exchanged for goods or services before the expiry date.

Your vouchers will be dispatched to you today and should reach you within two working days. Telephone our Customer Services staff on 0800 470033, quoting your reference number 8611680, if you have any queries.

Yours sincerely

Claire Pidgeon
Voucher Scheme Manager

Top + 2 please. One for Florence McDougall and one for our files. Indicate routing.

EXAM WP 2.B

Recall the information sheet stored as LIGHTING. Amend as shown. Change to double linespacing (except where indicated). Adjust left margin to 7cm and the top margin to 4 cm. Use full justification. Save as LIGHTING1 and print one copy.

LIGHTING YOUR HOME

Changing your lighting is important

~~This information sheet will help you with selecting lamps~~ either when decorating a new room or remodelling an old one. It has the power not only to give you the light source you need for everyday activities but to add to your home a variety of moods. Our lighting consultants are available to help with any questions you may have.

copy this sentence to point marked (A)

It is easy to become overwhelmed by the different designs that are available. Do not put in new lighting or a new ornamental lamp to then find that it does not fit in with your existing decoration. for any electrical sockets

Check the room before you buy a new ornamental lamp. Utilise the new lighting to enhance your existing furniture and décor. Take your time to do some research.

(B)

(Page 2 starts here)

It can be a cheap way of modernising your home.

Adding an extra ornamental lamp is often not in some rooms a feasible option such as bathrooms or kitchens // Think about the mood you want to convey from your lighting. Then think about whether the function of the light is for general lighting, task lighting or accent lighting

this section of text only in single linespacing

For general lighting purposes, whatever the room, recessed lighting ~~appears appropriate~~ seems popular. It gives a relaxed atmosphere and is useful if there is limited space. (✓)

The next function of interior lighting is task lighting. Task lighting is known to provide lighting for household duties such as cooking, cleaning, reading and working.

Last but not least there is accent lighting

~~One important function must be to highlight features~~. Accent lighting is designed to brighten up a particular feature. This could be a picture or an architectural feature. It is an easy ~~and relatively cheap~~ way of updating your home.

Page 3 starts here

KITCHEN LIGHTING

Inset this paragraph 4cm from left margin

Ceiling lighting can be important in a kitchen because there are so many different needs. As a great source of light consider using fluorescent fixtures which will also help save on energy bills. Down lighters mounted off the edge of cabinets are an excellent way to create additional lighting.

To help prevent shadows on the worktops consider the use of lights under cabinets. In open areas such as over sinks, use recessed downlighters mounted directly over the sink. Illuminate particular areas such as any architectural detail or eating areas with recessed or track lighting. Directional lighting will cast light on just the right places in your kitchen.

(A) Move to point marked (B)

The kitchen is often the busiest part of the house.

Do not rely on natural light from your windows to provide all your lighting. It is surprising how often you need extra light, especially in a kitchen, even in the middle of the day.

Insert LIGHTING INFORMATION to appear as a header at the right margin on every page

Number the pages ensuring that Page 1 is not numbered

Change ornamental to decorative throughout this document

Recall the advertisement stored as ADVERT.
Amend as shown. Save as ADVERTI. Print
a copy in landscape on one sheet of A4 paper.

LOW VOLTAGE LIGHTING

Each light comes with a health and safety leaflet.

These lights always stay cool and can be used safely in close proximity to furnishings.

They are safe with children and are more reliable than
traditional fairy lights and are cheaper to run. In the home,
if used imaginatively, they can create wonderful features.
Indoor and outdoor lights are available.

Their traditional use was at Christmas but more and
more people are using them all the year round.

This section only in a larger font size

Our most popular lights include:

Christmas tree
Cherry blossom tree
Ropes
Curtains
Flowers
Icicles
Fairy
Nets

Please sort into exact alphabetical order

Insert the picture
here stored as
FLOWERS. Change
measurement to
2.5 cm wide with
the text wrapped
to the left of the
picture.

on how they can be used

To give you fresh ideas come and see our display at the Lighting Exhibition which is being
held between 3 and 16 October at the New Town Hall, Stoke Street.

Every weekend there will be a permanent display at The Malthouse. Centre this sentence

Visit our website at www.maltlights.co.uk to see our
latest product range and place an order.

On completion, ensure you have saved your work and then
use your software facilities to perform a word count.
Key in this figure on a separate line below the final
line of text.

Recall the document stored as OFFERS. Amend as shown. Retain the Arial 11 font throughout the document. Save as OFFERS1 and print one copy.

LIGHTS ON OFFER

The following lights are some of the lines now on offer at a substantial discount. These are end of lines and none of the stock is faulty in any way. All purchases come with a 2-year guarantee and a health and safety leaflet.

DESCRIPTION	CODE	CONCESSIONARY PRICES	
		PERCENTAGE DISCOUNT	COST (£) INCLUDING VAT

CHRISTMAS AND SPECIAL OCCASIONS

Waterfall with star	WS2	50	79.95
Christmas conifer	CC23	22	36.00
Illuminated tree	TT6	30	59.00
White and blue icicles	WB9	18	9.35

AVAILABLE ALL THE YEAR ROUND

Blue and white battery	BB3	37	4.55
Red pyracantha	RP6	50	9.50
Magenta nets	MN8	35	25.50
Lavender curtains	LC2	20	30.00
Butterfly (pink or white)	PB7	25	14.50
Connectable rope	CR5	24	19.95

Leave a vertical space of at least 7.5cm here

Offers are changed on a regular basis. Visit our website at www.maltlights.co.uk to see our latest product range and to place an order. Availability is dependent on our suppliers.

Modify layout so that PERCENTAGE DISCOUNT becomes the last column.

Please sort PERCENTAGE DISCOUNT column into exact numerical order within each section starting with the highest number first. Ensure all corresponding details are also rearranged.

Recall the letterhead template stored as GREEN and key in the following document. Insert the autotext phrases as indicated. Use Comic Sans MS 12 font style for the letter but do not change the letterheading. Use full justification. Save as GREEN1 and print.

Our Ref JH/345

Mrs Nadia Jones
78 Fell Road
SHEFFIELD
S17 4JK

Top + 2 copies please. One for Kate Mosto and one for our files. Indicate routing.

Dear Mrs Jones

Thank you for your queries about buying one of our greenhouses. I agree that it is difficult to choose from so many styles and sizes.

If you decide to buy one of our greenhouses we will free of charge

Insert Autotext Phrase stored as FE2

For buildings over £5000 we will do all the construction work. This includes

• taking down any existing structures
• putting in any foundations and constructing the building
• carrying out all electrical work including lighting and power points and also doing any plumbing work.

Individual quotations are given for each type of work. This helps you choose the service you require us to do.

It may help you to decide on the size and type of greenhouse if you come and see our display of timber and aluminium structures. This is being held at River Field Showground from 1 February to 1 July. There are over 20 greenhouses of different designs on show and also a display of equipment such as staging, propagators and smaller items such as soft horticultural fleece. A consultant is always on site to offer advice.

Insert Autotext Phrase stored as FS2

EXAM WP 2.C

> Recall the information sheet stored as DETAILS. Amend as shown. Change to double linespacing (except where indicated). Adjust left margin to 4 cm and the top margin to 4.5 cm. Use full justification. Save as DETAILS2 and print one copy.

PROGRESS PROPERTIES

Progress Properties started in business

> and our attention to the environment

~~Our company was set up by John Davidson~~ almost 15 years ago and we now enjoy international recognition. Last year we won the coveted Builder of the Year Award. We are particularly well-known for the quality of our properties. Read on to see why you can trust Progress.

When you choose a Progress home you can rest assured that you are in safe hands. → *copy this sentence to point marked (*)*

NEW DEVELOPMENTS

There are currently 120 developments in progress across the UK and mainland Europe. These range from modern estates of 100 plots to small apartment developments. *For your closest new build, log on to our website. There you will find a location map, a site plan and a description of the properties, along with their prices.*

Contracts can be exchanged within four weeks. For a stress-free move, please check out our website for full details of how to make an application. It really could not be easier. → *move to point marked (*)(*)*

ECO-FRIENDLY OPTIONS

a full range of

Some of our newest builds include properties with/eco-friendly options. These include solar panels for low cost heating and triple insulation of floors and walls. [Some of our properties also have the option of rooftop planting. This offers a rainwater harvesting system which collects water. The water can be used in flushing toilets.

We can also offer automatic shutters to stop the properties getting too hot in the summer months.

> Page 2 starts here

PART-EXCHANGE SCHEME

very hard

In the current climate, it is often ~~quite difficult~~ to sell your house at a reasonable price. Under this scheme, we value your property and offer you the current market value. All you have to do is find the difference between the cost of your property and the price of your new Progress house. We do all the paper work. ✓

(*)(*) > That is why we offer our part-exchange scheme.

> Change house to home throughout this document

This paragraph only in single linespacing

Inset this paragraph 3 cm from left margin

FIRST TIME BUYERS

Most of our new developments include properties designed to appeal to the first time buyer. Not only do they offer modern, open plan living spaces, they are also fully equipped with kitchen appliances and basic lounge and bedroom furniture. Again, this makes for a simple move without all the additional costs involved in fitting out a new house.

(Page 3 starts here)

CONTACT US

If you would like more information about

~~For further details and descriptions of~~ any of our developments or if you wish to speak to a member of our sales team, please get in touch. Our telephone number is 024 7647 0033.

Our lines are open (every day) from 10 am until 5 pm ~~except on Sundays~~. We look forward to hearing from you.

Stop Press! We have some fantastic properties which have been reduced by 30%. Call us for details of these brilliant deals!

Insert INFORMATION SHEET to appear as a header at the right margin on every page

Number the pages ensuring that Page 1 is not numbered

> Recall the notice stored as RENTAL. Amend as shown. Save as RENTAL2. Print a copy in landscape on one sheet of A4 paper.

This paragraph only in a larger font size

PROPERTIES TO RENT

If you are wondering where to spend your holiday this year, why not consider joining us at The Haven, our new development on the edge of Lake Marvel?

purchase and

This apartment complex comprises properties for rental. There is a health club, pub and convenience store on site. Located only 5 minutes' walk from the lake, The Haven is an ideal holiday choice.

The apartments offer identical accommodation. An open-plan sitting room adjoins a well-equipped kitchen. The double bedrooms have queen-sized beds and large fitted wardrobes. The luxury bathroom has a separate shower and a whirlpool bath. Rental prices start at £250 per week in the low season.

Each rental property ~~at The Haven~~ offers these facilities as standard:

Dishwasher
Automatic washing machine
Audio system
Towels and bedlinen
Television and DVD
Underfloor heating

> Sort into exact alphabetical order

Fuel and power costs are included in the rental price.

Our larger properties have attractive terraces with a barbecue area.

PROGRESS PROPERTIES – LIVE THE DREAM! ← Centre

> On completion, ensure you have saved your work and then use your software facilities to perform a word count. Key in this figure on a separate line below the final line of text.

> Insert the picture here stored as LAKE. Change measurement to 6 cm wide with the text wrapped to the right of the picture.

Recall the document stored as EXPENSES. Amend as shown. Retain the Arial 11 font throughout the document. Save as EXPENSES2 and print one copy.

THE COST OF BUYING YOUR NEW HOME

The following table outlines the costs involved in the purchase of a new home. These expenses can add up to £4,000 to the purchase price. This can come as an unpleasant surprise for the inexperienced buyer. If you buy a Progress property, these expenses are forgotten because our prices are all-inclusive!

ITEM OF EXPENDITURE	ITEM CODE	FURTHER DETAILS	
		OPTIONAL EXPENSE?	APPROX COST £
POSSIBLE COSTS INCURRED AFTER PURCHASE			
Oven, hob and microwave	F78	Yes	350.00
Television and DVD player	F14	Yes	495.00
Washing machine	F74	Yes	250.00
Refrigerator and freezer	F72	Yes	200.00
EXPENSES INCURRED PRIOR TO PURCHASE			
Solicitors' fees (basic service)	E23	No	750.00
Money transfer fee	E26	No	25.50
Property survey (basic)	E51	No	350.00
Mortgage arrangement fee	E25	No	400.00
Bankruptcy search	E17	No	7.50

Leave a vertical space of at least 5 cm here

The above costs are based upon a property valued at £200,000. They do not include stamp duty.

Modify layout so that EXPENSES INCURRED PRIOR TO PURCHASE comes before POSSIBLE COSTS INCURRED AFTER PURCHASE section

Please sort APPROX COST £ column into exact numerical order within each section starting with the highest number first. Ensure all corresponding details are also rearranged.

Recall the letterhead template stored as PROPERTIES and key in the following document. Insert the autotext phrases as indicated. Use Trebuchet MS 12 font style for the letter but do not change the letterheading. Use a ragged right margin. Save as PROPERTIES2 and print.

Our ref   JL/ENQ

Mr and Mrs H Fretwell
65 Nelson Road
BANBURY
OX16 3DM

Top + 2 copies please. One for Mark Wilson and one for our files. Indicate routing.

Dear Mr and Mrs Fretwell

Thank you for your recent enquiry about our new building developments in the West Midlands. We are pleased to inform you that we are just finishing some new townhouses on the outskirts of Leamington Spa. I enclose a brochure giving details of the homes and their exact location.

When you have studied the brochure, please contact me if you would like to arrange a guided viewing. There has been much interest in these properties. I would therefore urge you not to wait too long before making a decision.

This particular development offers

Insert Autotext Phrase stored as FTR

These homes are eco-friendly. The solar thermal panels in the roof generate hot water, the properties are triple glazed and floors and walls alike are well insulated.

What is more, all Progress properties benefit from
- special deals for first time buyers
- a ten-year builders' warranty
- great rates on home and contents insurance premiums
- attractive landscaped gardens for outdoor dining and well-maintained communal grounds

Prices range from £175,000 to under £350,000.

Insert Autotext Phrase stored as DIS

I look forward to hearing from you.

Yours sincerely

Jed Lowe
Marketing Executive

AUDIO-TRANSCRIPTION LEVEL 2 PRACTICE EXAMS

WITH HINTS SHEETS COVERING

- Skills checklist
- General hints
- Hints for each document

HINTS FOR EXAM WORK: OCR AUDIO-TRANSCRIPTION LEVEL 2

Checklist of skills

You need to be able to carry out the following before you attempt the practice exams:

- use the audio equipment provided by your centre
- recall a letterhead or memo heading into your file
- lay out a letter
- lay out a memo/advertisement/notice
- alter linespacing
- allocate vertical space
- emphasise and underline text and headings
- correct words in text as dictated
- create new paragraphs
- present information in tables format
- format numbered paragraphs
- incorporate information announced during the exam
- indicate enclosure(s)
- indicate routing of extra copies
- add automatic page numbering.

General

- Start a **New** file for each document.
- Use either the **Header** or **Footer** facility to record your name, centre number and document number (together with automatic page numbering on any multi-paged document) on each printout.
- Use **Insert** to recall a letterhead template into your own new file, then use **Save As** to give it a file name. The templates are available on the Hodder Plus website.
- Thereafter click on the **Save** screen icon frequently as you work.

- Dictation for the exam documents is also available on the Hodder Plus website.
- Carry out dictated editing instructions as you key in.
- As you key in an email or internet address, your computer changes the text colour to blue and underscores it. It can be left like this but, if you wish, you may alter it by marking it then selecting **Format** → **Font** → **Underline** (none) → **Colour** (black).
- A Candidate Information Sheet is included with each exam. This lists addresses, references and proper nouns. Take care to copy these correctly as the words may be unfamiliar to you.
- You may print as often as you wish, both during and immediately after the exam time allocation.
- Once you have completed a document, replay the tape, listening carefully and checking that the hard copy is correct.
- **Ensure you have SAVED your final edited version of each document before you log off at the end of the session.**

Document 1: letter

- This document must be printed on the OCR letterhead template.
- It must be dated with the date on which you are doing the practice exam.
- Key in the *Our ref* as dictated. Do not add your own initials or insert a *Your ref*.
- Key the special mark immediately before the name and address.
- Key in text, making amendments as dictated.
- Follow capitalisation for the heading and text in the body of the letter as dictated.
- When underlining text, ensure that the line does not overshoot either end of the relevant text. It may include any punctuation that is part of the final word.
- If the document runs to more than a single page, the continuation sheet must be numbered. Use **Insert** → **Page Numbers** to customise your numbering. Single sheets should not be numbered.
- Indicate any enclosure(s) mentioned in the body of the letter by using *Enc/Encs* or *Att/Atts*.
- To route extra copies, key the routing information on the document and print three copies. Tick in pen against the name on one copy, and against *File* on the other copy. Routing may also be shown by using a symbol, e.g. √, → or by emboldening, underscoring or highlighting. Pencil marks are not acceptable.
- You may print extra copies and make routing ticks outside the exam time allocation, but you may not key in the copy details at that stage.
- Proofread carefully, using the **Spellcheck**, and check that you have not omitted or misplaced text.

Document 2: memo/advertisement/notice

- A memo must be dated with the date on which you are doing the practice exam. Do not date an advertisement or notice.
- In a memo, key in the *Our ref* as dictated. Do not add your own initials or insert a *Your ref*.
- Key in text, making amendments as dictated.
- Follow capitalisation for the heading and text in the body of the document as dictated.
- When emphasising a sentence or paragraph you may embolden, capitalise, underline, alter font style/size, centre or inset. Remember to take the emphasis instruction off at the end of the portion of text.
- When numbering paragraphs or items, you can key the numbers as you go, using the tab key to align the following text, or you can use **Format → Bullets and Numbering** → select **Numbered**, which will automatically align the text.
- Proofread carefully, using the **Spellcheck**, and check that you have not omitted or misplaced text.

Document 3: report/article

- Key in text, making amendments as dictated.
- Follow capitalisation for the heading and text in the body of the letter as dictated.
- When altering the linespacing of paragraphs of text, ensure that the linespacing between the paragraphs and before and after that section is consistent. Do not forget to change back at the end of the section.
- If the document runs to more than a single page, the continuation sheet must be numbered. Use **Insert → Page Numbers** to customise your numbering.
- This is the document in which to insert the extra text that is on the enclosed 'Instructions for Invigilator' sheet. In a live exam, this will be announced early on. The dictator will tell you exactly where to insert it.
- This document will include a table. Column widths are dictated for candidates keying the table using the tab key. The following hints apply to those using the tables function.

Displaying tabular work using tables function

- Work in *Print Layout View*.
- Key each line horizontally and use the tab key or cursors to move between cells.
- Column widths can easily be altered by dragging the column borders using your mouse.

- Extra linespaces can be inserted by pressing **Enter** from within the cell.
- Gridlines may be used in the table, but a clear linespace should be left below the column headings. Do not leave empty cells.
- To stop the gridlines from printing use **Format** → **Borders and Shading** → **Borders** → select **None**.
- Proofread carefully, using the **Spellcheck**, and check that you have not omitted or misplaced text.

Accessing audio practice exams material

Candidate Information Sheets and Instructions to Invigilator

Candidate Information Sheets and Instructions to Invigilator follow for these practice exams:

- AT 2.A – documents 1, 2 and 3
- AT 2.B – documents 1, 2 and 3
- AT 2.C – documents 1, 2 and 3.

Templates

The letter and memo templates are available on the Hodder Plus website at **www.hodderplus.co.uk/ocrtextprocessing**. The same templates can be used for each exam.

Dictated documents

The dictation for the above exams is also available on the Hodder Plus website.

EXAM AT 2.A

DOCUMENT 1

CANDIDATE INFORMATION SHEET

Included in dictation:

Henry Gupta

Kathleen Walters
Claims Manager

Anne Collins

Address:

5 Hazel Grove
BASINGSTOKE
Hampshire
RG24 9NR

Reference(s):

KL/BG

NB: All other instructions (eg courtesy titles, headings etc) will be given in the dictation.

DOCUMENT 2

CANDIDATE INFORMATION SHEET

Included in dictation:

Mark Collins

Address:

/

Reference(s):

/

NB: All other instructions (eg courtesy titles, headings etc) will be given in the dictation.

2

CANDIDATE INFORMATION SHEET

DOCUMENT 3

Included in dictation:

References:

Address:

NB: All other instructions (eg courtesy titles, special mark, extra copies, headings etc) will be given in the dictation.

INSTRUCTIONS FOR INVIGILATOR

DOCUMENT 3

About 15 – 30 minutes after the start of the examination, announce that for Document 3:

For the profit sharing scheme staff will need to have worked for the company for a minimum of two years in order to qualify.

EXAM AT 2.B

CANDIDATE INFORMATION SHEET

DOCUMENT 1

Included in dictation:

Jeffrey Thornton
Progress
Acme Insurance
Mike Deakin
Customer Services Manager
Renewals Department

References:

MD/PD

Address:

19 Purbeck Street
SWINDON
SN2 1AX

NB: All other instructions (eg courtesy titles, special mark, extra copies,
         headings etc) will be given in the dictation.

CANDIDATE INFORMATION SHEET

DOCUMENT 2

Included in dictation:

Progress
Victorian
Edwardian

References:

Address:

NB: All other instructions (eg courtesy titles, special mark, extra copies,
headings etc) will be given in the dictation.

CANDIDATE INFORMATION SHEET

DOCUMENT 3

Included in dictation:

Progress Conference Centre
Newport
Ryde
Sandown
Ventnor
Cowes
Yarmouth
English
Continental

References:

Address:

NB: All other instructions (eg courtesy titles, special mark, extra copies,
         headings etc) will be given in the dictation.

DOCUMENT 3

INSTRUCTIONS TO INVIGILATOR:

About 15-30 minutes after the start of the examination, announce that for

Document 3:

it is proud to be ranked among the top one hundred centres in the country.

EXAM AT 2.C

CANDIDATE INFORMATION SHEET

Included in dictation:

Mr Norman Jacques

024 7647 0033

Trevor Eaton

Mark Stevens

References:

TE/BW

Address:

78 Manor Road

COLWYN BAY

LL28 4XY

NB: All other instructions (eg courtesy titles, department names, headings etc) will
        be given in the dictation.

CANDIDATE INFORMATION SHEET

Included in dictation:

Christopher Miller
Delia Watson

References:

DW/KL

Address:

NB: All other instructions (eg courtesy titles, department names, headings etc) will
be given in the dictation.

CANDIDATE INFORMATION SHEET

Included in dictation:

Progress Holiday Lettings

Cornwall

Cornish

024 7647 0033

www.progresslettings.com

References:

Address:

NB: All other instructions (eg courtesy titles, department names, headings etc) will be given in the dictation.

INSTRUCTIONS FOR INVIGILATOR

About 15-30 minutes after the start of the examination, announce that for Document 3 properties are available for short term or long term rental.

WORKED EXAMPLES

5

This section provides worked examples of each practice exercise and exam in this book.

The worked examples show one way of displaying the material, but this will not be the only acceptable way. For example, you may have decided to use different emphasis, your line ends may differ slightly or you may have left extra linespacing after headings. This is acceptable as long as you have followed instructions and formatted your document consistently.

To get the most from the worked examples, carry out each practice exercise or complete exam, then proofread it before referring to this chapter to check your work.

The workings of each set of exercises and exams for each different unit are grouped together, as follows:

- Text Production practice exercises – TP 2.1 to TP 2.15
- Text Production practice exams – TP 2.A, TP 2.B, TP 2.C
- Word Processing practice exercises – WP 2.1 to WP 2.18
- Word Processing practice exams – WP 2.A, WP 2.B, WP 2.C
- Audio-Transcription practice exercises – AT 2.1 to AT 2.15
- Audio-Transcription practice exams – AT 2.A, AT 2.B, AT 2.C.

Progress Group
Westwood Way
Coventry
CV4 8JQ

024 7647 0033

Our ref WB/hm

10 January 2009

PRIVATE AND CONFIDENTIAL

Mr K Rowe
10 Sherwood Avenue
CALNE
Wiltshire
SN11 3GE

Dear Mr Rowe

Thank you for coming into this branch to discuss a bank loan. As agreed the money will be paid into your current account on Wednesday 4 February 2009 and you will be able to withdraw this money the following day.

Repayments will be in six instalments and will be taken directly from your account. I have pleasure in enclosing the repayment plan. Please contact me if you have any questions about your loan.

I would like to take this opportunity to give you details about our range of credit cards. The interest rate on all our cards is <u>very low</u>. As well as paying for miscellaneous items using your credit card you can also obtain cash. As you are an existing customer and you are in employment you would be able to get a credit card very quickly. It is possible to transfer all of your outstanding balances from other credit and store cards in order to pay a lower interest rate. If you would like any further information please let me know.

Thank you for your custom in the past. I look forward to meeting you again in the future.

Yours sincerely

Wendy Barlow
Loan Manager

Enc

TEXT PRODUCTION EXERCISE TP 2.2: WORKED EXAMPLE

PROGRESS ACADEMY
Stirling Way
READING
RG3 7YC

Telephone 0118 233 4343

Our ref   TR/SPT

Day month year

BY HAND

Mrs R Walters
54 Main Street
CHIEVELEY
RG17 6PG

Dear Mrs Walters

Thank you for your cheque for £100 which is the deposit for your daughter's forthcoming school trip to Spain. I enclose a receipt. Please note that the <u>balance of £250</u> is due on Monday Day Month.

As discussed at our recent meeting, I confirm that group members will meet in the school hall on the day before departure so that travel documents can be checked by members of staff. A coach has been hired to take everyone to the airport so there is no need for parents to be concerned about transport. On our return, the coach will bring everyone back to school. You are warmly invited to collect your daughter. We will let you know our time of arrival.

The staff believe that this visit will be very beneficial to all students, particularly those who are getting ready for their final examinations. It will offer learners the chance to put their language skills into practice. They will also be able to experience Spanish culture at first hand.

I am sure that your daughter will enjoy herself and I would like to take this opportunity to thank you for your financial support.

Yours sincerely

Toni Ramirez
Head of Languages

Enc

TEXT PRODUCTION EXERCISE TP 2.3 WORKED EXAMPLE

Progress Group
180 Leopold Road
MULBARTON
Norfolk
NR14 9HZ

01508 777656

Our Ref   JG/AB

BY HAND

Day Month Year

Mr P McNaughton
246 Chaucer Square
Intwood Park
NORWICH
NR4 7YZ

Dear Mr McNaughton

This is to confirm our telephone conversation this morning. As discussed, we will start work on your art studio on Monday (Day Month).

Building regulations require an inspection of the foundations. Weather permitting, we will aim to dig these out ready for approval on the Tuesday. Hardwood doors and window frames can be measured up once the bricks have been laid. An order for the woodwork can then be put in.

For security reasons we plan to complete all the external work before taking down the existing wall between your entrance porch and the new building.

We estimate that, from start to finish, the work will take about 6 weeks. Meanwhile you can think about choosing the fixtures and fittings. Once the concrete floor and plasterwork have fully dried out, the room can be decorated with your choice of paint and emulsion. Worktops, cupboards, shelves, etc can then be fitted.

As agreed, you will make <u>direct payment </u>to the plumber and electrician. An allowance for this was shown on the estimate sent to you earlier this year.

We look forward to completing this work to our usual high standard and on time.

Yours sincerely

Jack Gorringe
Site Manager

MEMORANDUM

To   All Department Heads

From   Martin Perry, Office Manager

Date   5 January 2009

Ref   MP/hs

Next month there will be a health and safety inspection, so please refer to the booklet I sent to you last year for the details.

One of my main concerns is items of equipment and furniture left in corridors. As you know there is a large storage area in the basement. If you need the keys to the basement I will arrange to let you have access.

The enclosed form requires your signature. The form states that you will act on this by the end of the month so please let me know if you have any questions.

Enc

MEMORANDUM

To   Matt Robinson

From   Tom Brennan

Date   Day Month Year

Ref   TB/JEN

Mrs Jenkins of 15 Brackley Crescent has been in touch with us again. Her 32 inch plasma television needs further attention. This is the third time she has contacted us recently. The television keeps losing its satellite channels and cannot be re-tuned automatically. Our engineers cannot resolve the problem.

I have spoken to Roger and we have agreed that the best way forward is to recall the television and return it to the manufacturer. Mrs Jenkins is very happy with this decision. Please ask Sanjay to deliver a replacement set to her tomorrow morning. All the details are in the client file.

M E M O R A N D U M

To: Amelia Ayton

From: James Ricard

Date: Day Month Year

Ref: JR/MSS

I received a telephone call this morning from Julie Lardent about her application for the administrative assistant vacancy in our accounts section. It appears that the Job Description was not enclosed in the information pack we sent her last week. I suggest that we email her a copy today as this will save time.

We have so far received a number of applications for this post. We should compile a shortlist of candidates in the near future. References can then be taken up before the interviews are held. A definite date must be set aside for these within the next two weeks.

PRESS RELEASE

Company Name   Progress Department Store

Contact Person   Beverly Ford

Date   Day Month Year

Progress Department Store is pleased to announce the opening of a new store in Bristol.

As this store will be approximately double the size of the current one we will need to employ more staff. We require permanent staff and temporary staff next season. We will start holding interviews next week. Please telephone if you would like an application form.

Everyone is welcome to come to the opening where there will be many free gifts. There will also be many bargains and with the help of our staff we are sure the new store will be a great success.

PRESS RELEASE

Company Name	Progress Electronics
Contact Person	Damyanti Pattni, Human Resources Assistant
Date	Day Month Year

Progress Electronics is pleased to announce the planned construction of a second factory in South Wales.

The business has enjoyed a surge in popularity over recent years. Increased demand for its products has led to the decision to expand the company's workforce. It is believed the new building will be ready in two years' time. Approximately 500 staff will be employed on the new site.

In response to this news, City analysts predict that Progress Electronics will continue to lead the way in Britain's fast-moving and innovative electronics industry. As a result, share prices have risen by 15 per cent.

TEXT PRODUCTION EXERCISE TP 2.9: WORKED EXAMPLE

PRESS RELEASE

Company Name   Progress Banking Group

Contact Person   Christa Weiss

Date   Day Month Year

Progress Banking Group is delighted to announce the launch of two new internet only accounts. These will be offered to personal customers with immediate effect.

The online saver account can be opened with as little as £1. A fixed rate of interest is guaranteed for the first year.

The other new online account is a cash individual savings account. This is tax free and may be opened with £10. Customers can save up to £3,600 each year free of tax.

Both new accounts provide greater convenience and flexibility and will help to reduce paper and postage. The environment should benefit as well.

FILE NOTE

From   Jennifer Poole

Position   Customer Services Manager

Date   10 January 2009

File Number 2027

Mrs Brooke bought conservatory blinds from this company last year. We gave a guarantee that the blinds would last for five years.

My secretary received a message from Mrs Brooke on Friday last week to say that one of her blinds was broken. I sent one of our inspectors to look at the problem. His report states that the fault is due to a badly stitched seam.

We will have to give Mrs Brooke a new blind but at present we do not have fabric in the colour to match available.

I have asked the quality control manager to review procedures.

FILE NOTE

From	Rekha Patel
Position	Training Manager
Date	Day Month Year
File Number	428

Today's meeting with the External Verifier went very well. All our portfolios were accepted. Jackie was extremely complimentary about the standard of work submitted. We will receive a copy of her report within the next few days.

The examinations board is planning to make some changes to the syllabus. Jackie has given us a copy of the new requirements. I intend to add this topic to the agenda for next week's meeting. We need to be clear how the changes will affect our organisation.

If possible, please look at the documents before we meet so that a full discussion can take place.

FILE NOTE

From:	Gemma Porter
Position:	Office Manager
Date:	Day Month Year
File Number:	61189

I spoke to Les Thompson, Recycling Officer, at County Hall with regard to collecting the furniture which is surplus to our requirements. He said that, for a small charge per item, this would be possible. The collection day in our area is a Wednesday. He asked us to make sure the items were left safely in full view before 7 am on the day in question.

I explained that we were expecting delivery of some new equipment. Upon receipt, we would request a collection date. He said they must have at least two weeks' notice.

I agreed to contact him in due course.

TEXT PRODUCTION EXERCISE TP 2.13: WORKED EXAMPLE

PROGRESS COTTAGE HOLIDAYS

Cottage holidays provide the best value for money. Some of our cottages are available for rent all year and some only during the summer months. We have all types of property on our books. You can choose flats in city centres or charming country houses. Whatever the size of your party we have accommodation to suit you.

Dogs are welcome in houses, chalets and cottages but in some cases there is a limit to the number of dogs allowed so please check when booking. Properties with fenced gardens are very suitable for dogs and in our catalogue we have listed all these properties in one section.

Discounts for Next Season

At the present time we are giving a discount for early bookings for next season. If you book two weeks with us you will receive a free gift.

Holidays by the Sea or in Rural Areas

Adults and children like walking, playing and sitting on the beach. We have many chalets close to the sea and these are very popular with young families.

On our books we have cottages in rural areas and if you enjoy nature, some of these properties will provide you with the perfect holiday.

More Houses Needed

We require more houses to rent as soon as possible. Please contact us immediately if you can help.

At Progress owners are paid good rates for holiday rentals. All we ask in return is that you keep the property maintained.

Owners have to arrange for cleaning to be carried out each week and all the gardens must be kept tidy.

We look after every one of our owners as we rely on them to provide an excellent service to our clients.

Some of our owners have more than one cottage to let. In many areas in this country landlords can make more money with holiday lettings than they can with residential lettings.

It is hard for an owner to let property without any help. We do all the advertising and we collect the deposits and other payments from clients.

We insist that clients take out insurance to cover accidental damage when staying in holiday homes. This policy has been written for us by an insurance company. Therefore we know that the cover is enough to protect our owners from any loss.

If you would like more details about letting your property we will be pleased to talk to you. Alternatively, you can go to our website where you will find further information.

2

TEXT PRODUCTION EXERCISE TP 2.14: WORKED EXAMPLE

PROGRESS GARDEN CENTRES

Progress Garden Centres have been in business since 1985 when Jean and Jack Denman started to develop their land as a nursery. Over the years, helped by their family and staff, the firm has grown. There are now nine garden centres across the West Midlands. Wherever you live within the region, you will not be far from one of our garden centres.

PLANTS AND SHRUBS

<u>From the outset Progress Garden Centres have been synonymous with quality</u>. Healthy plants and shrubs are grown on our premises. They are offered for sale at competitive prices. Attractive displays show just how easily the plants can be grown. More unusual species are imported from Europe.

ADVICE AND GUIDANCE

Our staff are all experienced garden experts. They are always happy to offer advice and guidance to customers. If you have a question, feel free to ask any member of staff as you wander around the centre. If the member questioned does not have an immediate answer, we will contact you with the response as soon as possible.

LECTURE PROGRAMME

Every Friday morning, our garden experts give lectures on a range of horticultural subjects. Each lecture lasts for approximately one hour and is free of charge. However, as our lecture rooms are quite small, please book in advance. You can do this by calling your nearest Progress Garden Centre or by going to our website and following the link.

2

GARDEN DESIGN

Running in conjunction with the nursery side of the business, we also run a garden design service. Our team of garden designers are fully qualified and have many years of experience between them.

If you wish to redesign your garden we can help. An initial visit to your garden and a full discussion of your ideas is offered free of charge. We will prepare a design and present it to you. If you like what we suggest, our design team will construct the garden on your behalf, undertaking the landscaping and planting for you. Prices start at £2000 for a small garden.

If you want to be fully involved in the transformation of your garden but need assistance with the planning process, we can work with you to produce plans. If you wish, we can draw up a planting diagram for you. This inexpensive service costs only £250 for an average garden.

CONTACT US

If you would like to visit one of our centres or use our garden design service, please visit our

website: www.progressgardens.co.uk. We look forward to meeting you!

TEXT PRODUCTION EXERCISE TP 2.15: WORKED EXAMPLE

YAREDALE PROTECTION SOCIETY

The following draft will form the basis of the Chairman's report at next month's meeting.

MEMBERSHIP

Our numbers have now dropped to around 300 households. Approximately half of these are life members; 30% have paid for 5 years and the rest pay their subscriptions annually.

PUBLIC LIABILITY INSURANCE

After a long debate it was agreed that, although costly for a group such as ours, public liability insurance should be taken out. This would cover us for guided walks along the valley and for any social functions that might be arranged during the year. It would also cover our Annual General Meeting.

FUTURE PROJECTS IN YAREDALE

Concern was expressed at the planning application for building 2 wind turbines in a lovely part of the valley. The society has no objection in principle to saving energy by building wind farms. **However, the siting of such a development is of prime importance.** A number of petitions from other groups, opposed to the project, had been sent in. As a result the request was withdrawn.

It was noted that planning permission for a leisure centre and retail outlet on land running down to the river had been refused.

2

YAREDALE WALKS BOOKLET

The committee agreed to update the current guide which had sold well. This would include the new boardwalk to the west of Yaredale. It is hoped to publish the new guide early next year. Advertisers will be approached to help offset some of the cost.

NEWSLETTERS

The Chairman expressed his thanks to Patsy Smith for overseeing the distribution of the newsletters. Once again the question of sending these online was brought up. However, it was agreed to continue to deliver them by hand for the time being.

CORRESPONDENCE

Several members have written to say that the footpath along the river is often flooded after heavy rain. Another member expressed concern over the amount of litter lying near the picnic tables close to the marshes. The Secretary has emailed the council about these matters.

Other correspondence received pointed out the danger of giant hogweed which has become a problem in the valley.

Planning information about new housing projects close to the river has also been received.

WEBSITE

The society is pleased to report that it now has a website. This includes some beautiful photographs of the valley taken during each season. New members can complete the membership form online. A token of appreciation has been sent to the designer.

Please email your comments to the Chairman as soon as possible.

TEXT PRODUCTION EXAM TP 2.A: WORKED EXAMPLE

Progress Group
Westwood Way
Coventry
CV4 8JQ

024 7647 0033

Our ref BA/cn

10 January 2009

BY HAND

Mrs D Richardson
56 Waterford Road
WELLING
Kent
DA16 2JB

Dear Mrs Richardson

Thank you for your recent order for a new greenhouse. We will be able to deliver this on Tuesday 10 February and your greenhouse will be built the same day. We will need to lay the concrete base at least five days before delivery. It is necessary to ensure that the concrete has had sufficient time to dry before building your greenhouse. Please contact my secretary in order to arrange a day and time to lay the base.

We have much pleasure in enclosing our latest catalogue giving details and prices of our greenhouse accessories. As you can see we sell a wide range of accessories in many sizes and colours. If you would like to order any of these items please let us know as soon as possible and we may be able to deliver them at the same time as your greenhouse.

All our greenhouses and other garden buildings come with a guarantee and we will send this to you at the end of next month.

We hope that you will enjoy growing plants in your new greenhouse. If you have any questions then please do not hesitate to contact us again.

Yours sincerely

Belinda Alison
Sales Manager

Enc

PRESS RELEASE

Company Name   Progress Builders

Contact Person   James Doyle

Date 10 January 2009

Progress Builders is pleased to offer a discount on any work undertaken within the next three months.

This is a good opportunity to get all those outstanding projects completed. We can give estimates immediately.

Discounts will be given on all types of building work. However large or small the job we know we can do the work to a very high standard.

All our workers are experts in their field and are experienced builders. As a result we are able to carry out loft conversions as well as building extensions.

If you would like any further information or an estimate please contact us.

OFFICE MOVE

This report is to be sent to all department heads who will then circulate to their staff. Everyone has to be aware of what needs to be done.

The lease on our current office space runs out at the end of next month. The directors have been looking at other premises in town. Last week a lease was signed on new office space. These new premises are in the High Street and will provide us with more space than we have currently.

Clearing of the Rubbish and Packing Boxes

Next Friday there will be a rubbish collection. Staff must label items for disposal and these should include any broken electrical equipment, desks and chairs.

It should be noted that all documents must be shredded before being put into the paper recycling sacks. Further supplies of these sacks have been bought, and will be available soon.

Old data disks must be placed in the boxes supplied. These will be given to a specialist company. All data on the disks will be wiped and then the disks will be destroyed.

All department heads will be attending a meeting to discuss the best layout for the new offices. When this has been done the layout will be made available to all members of staff.

It will be necessary for staff to spend at least two hours each week helping to pack items into boxes. A rota will be arranged for this purpose. It may be that we will have to spend more or less time on packing. We can assess this again soon.

Please let your manager know if you are willing to work overtime in order to help with the packing.

The week before the move the removal men will issue us with numbered labels. These labels should be put on chairs, desks and cabinets. The numbers will correspond with the new office plan. The removal men will therefore be able to place all items in the correct rooms.

In order that the office continues to run smoothly the move will take place over the course of a week. This means that only one department at any time will be disrupted.

Prospects for the Future

The directors are sure that the new offices will enable us to expand our business and extra space will allow us to diversify and employ more staff.

We are looking forward to the move and we know that our staff will do what they can to help make this a huge success.

TEXT PRODUCTION EXAM TP 2.B: WORKED EXAMPLE

PROGRESS CARS
Westwood Way
COVENTRY
CV4 8JQ

Telephone 024 7647 0033

Our ref JF/EN43

Day Month Year

PRIVATE AND CONFIDENTIAL

Mr Martin Reid
Technotrial Limited
64 Humberstone Road
BIRMINGHAM
B2 6XJ

Dear Martin

Thank you for your letter enquiring about the benefits of adopting a car share scheme for your employees. I am pleased to hear that you are thinking of reviewing your company's business mileage.

Car share schemes are becoming very popular throughout the United Kingdom. Many people believe that it is a greener alternative to owning a car. It is also less expensive. Some schemes, like ours, require clients to settle their account monthly. You pay only for your mileage, plus a daily or hourly rental fee.

In Birmingham we have a network of dedicated car share spaces. We guarantee that there will be an available vehicle within 10 minutes' walk of your office. There are approximately 150 parking spaces devoted to our cars. Reserve your car online or by telephone.

If you would like to discuss the matter further, please telephone to arrange an appointment. In the meantime, I enclose our latest information sheet. We are currently offering new business clients <u>a 20% discount</u> if they register before Friday Date Month.

I hope that you will use Progress Cars as your car share provider. I look forward to hearing from you.

Yours sincerely

Jason Fullhurst
Marketing Executive

Enc

FILE NOTE

From   Tanya Brown

Position   Evening Supervisor

Date   Day Month Year

File Number   49632

Yesterday Mr James Ecclestone telephoned. His customer reference is E19842. He would like his wife to be added to his membership. Her name is Andrea. She is an experienced driver and holds a clean British driving licence.

Unfortunately when he called the client database was being tested. I did not have an opportunity to update his records. Mr Ecclestone's details need to be amended urgently as his wife wishes to use a Progress car next week.

I have requested a smartcard in her name and it will be ready later today. Mrs Ecclestone will call in at the office to collect it.

CAR SHARING WITH PROGRESS CARS

Over recent years Progress Cars has been developing its car sharing scheme across the United Kingdom. With dedicated car spaces in more than ten cities, Progress now has more than 5000 clients. Read on to see how you could benefit from becoming a member of our club.

WHY SHARE?

Car sharing not only makes financial sense, it also helps the environment. For every car shared, it is estimated that six cars are taken off the road. Sharing a car means that you pay only when you need to make a journey. Costs such as road tax, insurance, repairs and depreciation are no longer an issue.

THE PRICE OF SHARING

It costs just £50 for an individual to join the club. Companies can register for £150 and this covers the subscription for up to ten members of staff. Membership is renewed annually. In addition, members pay a daily or hourly rate for the use of the vehicle. A 1.4 litre diesel hatchback costs £4 per hour or £40 for each 24-hour period. Larger vehicles and vans cost slightly more. For each day of the booking, you get 30 miles of free petrol. After that, mileage plus petrol is charged at 25p per mile.

HOW THE SCHEME WORKS

Whenever you wish to book a car, let us know by telephone or email. Tell us the type of vehicle required, the length of the booking and your preferred pick-up location. We will confirm by text message or email. We will indicate the make, colour and registration number of the car.

At the collection point, use your Progress smartcard to unlock the vehicle. Once inside, use the card to access the keys from the glove compartment. Enter your pin number onto the keypad on the dashboard and drive away.

On your return please leave the car in its designated space. Your account is payable at the end of the month.

2

BUSINESS CLIENTS

Progress Cars offers business clients all the advantages of operating a fleet of cars, but without the fixed costs and depreciation. If you use our cars on a daily basis, we can even locate our vehicles in your own office car park. For most organisations car sharing clubs work out cheaper than paying staff to use their own vehicle for business travel.

JOIN US NOW

To join our club, visit our website: www.progresscars.co.uk. Complete the online form with the necessary details. That is all it takes. We look forward to welcoming you to our club soon!

TEXT PRODUCTION EXAM TP 2.C: WORKED EXAMPLE

Progress Group
180 Leopold Road
MULBARTON
Norfolk
NR14 9HZ

01508 777656

Our ref   PB/MA

Day Month Year

CONFIDENTIAL

Ms Lucy Chaston
89 Wilmslow Crescent
BRACKEN ASH
Norfolk
NR14 6YA

Dear Lucy

As you know, our company is undergoing a period of major reorganisation. The aim is to streamline our operations in order to improve our efficiency. As a result, all staff are being asked to reapply for their jobs. The attached document outlines the posts in your section for which you can apply. Please tick 3 boxes indicating your preferred choice.

The application process is in 2 parts. Firstly, all employees <u>are obliged</u> to attend an assessment day. The date for this is shown on the enclosed information sheet. Secondly, a week or so later, interviews will be held. Your interview date is Thursday (day month) at 9.30 am at head office.

We appreciate that this is an anxious time for all staff. However, we do not expect any redundancies. Those employees nearing retirement will be offered a very tempting financial package. Other staff will be given jobs based on their performance on the assessment day and at interview. This whole process should be achieved within 3 months.

Our Chief Executive wishes to thank you all for your loyal commitment over many years and looks forward to working with you in the future.

Yours sincerely

Paul Bulmer
Director of Human Resources

Encs

MEMORANDUM

To: Frances Westwell

From: Fadil Mehta

Date: Day Month Year

Ref: FM/DAC

Our organisation, in common with other research institutes, is concerned at the current skills shortage in the field of horticulture.

With this in mind, we have agreed to man a stand at the local Careers Fair. This is to be held in the autumn. It would give us an opportunity to highlight the many career paths in horticulture open to people of all ages.

With your years of experience in this subject, I should be grateful if you would write a short article on A5 paper for this event. Please let me see a draft copy before the end of next week.

A CAREER IN HORTICULTURE

Horticulture is defined as the art or science of growing garden plants. A career in this field can be varied and fulfilling. This vast industry is one of the largest employers in the British Isles, with jobs ranging from planting seeds to landscape design. Many of these involve working in the open air. Other openings are in garden centres where numerous opportunities are available for both skilled and unskilled workers.

GARDEN DESIGN

A career in garden design can be very rewarding. Students come from all walks of life and do not need experience in graphic art. All sizes of garden have to be planned and drawn to scale. Family gardens will include children's play areas and space for relaxation. If the garden is large enough, water features and fruit and vegetable plots may be built in.

Diploma courses are open to students of all ages and with no formal training. A passion for gardens is a key factor for a successful career in this field.

PARK RANGER

The duties of a park ranger are diverse. The main aims are to protect the park resources for the future and to look after its visitors. Some rangers provide a useful information service. This may include weather forecasts or the siting of a rare plant or bird. In addition, they might lead guided tours, deal with forest fires, rescue animals, etc. Education to degree level in a relevant subject is necessary. A good knowledge of trees and plants is recommended.

GREENKEEPER

If you enjoy sport and like outdoor life, then employment as a greenkeeper would be a healthy and satisfying career for you. Golf greenkeepers aim to provide the best playing conditions for club members and matches.

2

Training can be undertaken in the workplace. Assessment is carried out on the job

and can lead to a National Vocational Qualification. On the other hand, a National

Certificate can be achieved by attending a college course. This may be studied full

or part time for one or two years.

GARDEN CENTRE CAREERS

Garden centres provide good career paths in many miscellaneous jobs. These

include marketing, sales and management. For a junior post, a knowledge of plants

is vital. A horticultural qualification is also helpful. Senior posts would require a

degree in an appropriate subject, as well as experience in the chosen option.

Other options are in forestry, growing and developing seeds, floral work and

research. References to these and other careers in this industry can be found on the

Internet.

CHOOSING A FRANCHISE

Franchising is a term which is used to describe a type of business arrangement which is becoming increasingly popular. It involves the granting of a licence by one person (the franchisor) to another (the franchisee). This entitles the franchisee to trade under the brand established by the franchisor and to sell identical products or provide identical services.

With careful research a franchisee can become involved with a well-known brand at relatively low cost.

THE ADVANTAGES

This arrangement is ideal for people who would like to run their own business but do not have the funds or the experience to go it alone. A good franchise will offer a proven business format, along with guidance and support from the outset.

Investment costs range from as little as £5,000 for a share in a cleaning service to £250,000 for a franchise in a major fast food outlet.

The new investor will use the same proven systems as the main business, since these have been tried and tested. Therefore, the risks are fewer and the costs are much lower.

BUSINESS OPTIONS

2

When the agreement is finalised, the franchisee will often spend time working alongside the franchisor, to see exactly how the business works. Training will usually be given to improve knowledge and skill.

Continuing guidance will be given to ensure that the brand quality is upheld and the business remains profitable.

With careful research, a franchisee can become involved with a well-known brand at **relatively low cost.**

THE DISADVANTAGES

As with any business that is not entirely one's own, many franchisees feel frustrated that they cannot put their own stamp on the business. However, part of the agreement compels total adherence to the proven way of working, from the design of uniforms to the components used in the manufacturing process.

Another consideration, after the initial financial investment, is the payment of fees on the profits made. Whilst the franchise agreement is in force, the franchisee is compelled to pay fees to the franchisor.

EUROPEAN CODE OF ETHICS FOR FRANCHISING

The European Franchise Federation (EFF) was set up to promote the franchise industry in general and its members' interests in particular.

In 1989, after consultation with franchise organisations in 10 European countries, it reviewed its Code of Ethics. This exists to support the ethical conduct of all business relating to franchising and is a useful source of reference for those who involve themselves in a franchise agreement.

BUSINESS OPTIONS

3

MORE INFORMATION

To learn more about franchising, contact the British Franchise Association. They offer free advice and guidance on how to get the best out of setting up a franchise opportunity. Check out their website for ways to limit your risk!

BUSINESS OPTIONS

WORD PROCESSING EXERCISE WP 2.2: WORKED EXAMPLE

VEGETABLE PLANTING

CROP ROTATION

Farmers have always followed the practice of crop rotation. This is a system of regularly changing the crops grown on a piece of land. The crops are grown in a particular order to utilise and add to the nutrients in the soil and to control contamination by pests and diseases.

A typical rotation may consist of grass or potatoes followed by a wheat crop and then one of barley. In this way, the cereal crops take advantage of the build-up of soil fertility which occurs during the period under grass. The quality of the ground dictates whether there will be one or two crops of wheat and barley.

In modern farming, the potato or grass crop may be replaced with a forage crop such as maize. The heavy use of manure required for this crop ensures that two crops of wheat and two crops of barley can be grown easily in following years.

VEGETABLE PLANTING

Vegetables definitely benefit from being grown in soil that has not been used for the same crop the previous year.

Different plants need different growing conditions so soil type needs to be established. It is important to distinguish between the acid or alkaline content.

Decide on the conditions needed for each crop to ensure optimum growth and yield. Some crops prefer a neutral to acid soil whereas others thrive in an alkaline soil.

The beds should be dug over thoroughly and fertilised. Lime should be added to produce the correct alkaline level.

Gardeners can follow the same principles of crop rotation when growing vegetables. Follow the basic rule of not planting the same crop in the same place for more than one year at a time.

VEGETABLE PLANTING

Divide the growing area into four beds. Some crops such as rhubarb, strawberries, raspberries, all fruit trees and asparagus can be grown in the same position each year. The area where these crops will be planted will be a permanent bed. It should be thoroughly prepared before planting because it will not be rotated each year.

The remaining three beds would become part of a simple rotation. Different plants need different growing conditions so soil type needs to be established.

For the first year, root crops such as carrots, beetroot and parsnips can be planted in the first bed. In the second year, this bed would contain potatoes and tomatoes. In the third year, cabbages, cauliflowers, broccoli and sprouts could be planted.

Gardeners often have limited space available so this simple rotation system is effective. With more space, the rotation system can be extended to four or five years. The longer the ground is given to recover between planting the same crop, the better the results will be.

WORD PROCESSING EXERCISE WP 2.3: WORKED EXAMPLE

SCHOOL PARTNERSHIPS

Over the last 3 years the company has developed a partnership with 5 local primary schools. Volunteers from our staff have been involved in a variety of projects. They have helped run activities such as vegetable gardening.

Jill Bacon co-ordinates the volunteers and liaises with the schools on a regular basis. The schools are very appreciative of the volunteers' help. It has been decided to continue these projects. The response from our staff has been excellent.

Pip North, headmistress of Lower Middleton Primary, suggested that because of our expertise we might consider sponsoring buying a small greenhouse which could be used for propagation. The pupils have tried growing seeds in the past but with little success. The school is sited on a very windy hill with poor soil and sowing seeds had been unsuccessful. The children have become disheartened. It was felt that it was important that the children see fairly fast results although also seeing failures.

Middleton School

FINANCE

These school projects have been funded from the Partnership Fund. Any donations from staff are matched by the company. It has been agreed that the company will top up the Fund by £1000 which will cover the initial costs so that other sponsorships are not affected.

VEGETABLES OR FLOWERS?

As part of their learning the children will take responsibility for deciding what crops to grow. Jill Bacon has contacted the local allotment society. The society has been very helpful. John Rivers, from the North Allotment Society, has produced a list of what should grow well. These include cabbages, courgettes, leeks, lettuce, peas, potatoes and radishes. It was felt that it was important that the children see fairly fast results although also seeing failures.

John has also produced a list of what does not grow well in this area which includes carrots and parsnips. He has agreed to be the school's vegetable consultant. This should be a useful contact for the school.

Care must be taken in ensuring that the vegetables are not ready in the summer holidays so it is important to research suitable varieties. The caretaker has agreed to do any watering that is required during weekends and holidays.

FUTURE DEVELOPMENTS

If any of the other schools want a greenhouse it should be possible to offer another 2 next year. It is hoped to gain valuable information from this project which can be used with the other schools.

SETTING UP

Jason Heath has agreed to liaise with the setting up of the greenhouse. It has been decided to put in staging at different heights so that children from various **age groups can use the greenhouse.** If money permits a cold frame will be purchased so gaining its full potential.

Middleton School

SLEEP EASY WITH PROGRESS

With almost 20% of the population suffering from a lack of sleep, it makes sense to try to alleviate the problem by making some changes. For some people, a change in lifestyle is required.   Too much activity close to bedtime can result in disrupted sleep patterns. A warm bath before bed may also be helpful. Alternatively, perhaps a change of bed is needed. That is where Progress can help!

Our Progress showrooms stock a range of beds that can make a big difference to the quality of your sleep.

TYPES OF BED

There are many different types and sizes of bed. You should be able to find one to suit your needs and your budget. Progress Beds come in 4 main sizes – single, double, queen (5 feet) and king (6 feet). Other widths can be ordered.

Lengths vary too. The standard length is 6 feet, but an additional 6 inches is usual on king-sized beds. Very tall people often request an even longer bed.

MATTRESSES

Sharing a bed with a partner does not necessarily mean that a mattress has to be shared too. Larger beds may have zipped mattresses. This means that each partner has a separate mattress (possibly of a different firmness) to suit their particular needs.   The mattresses are zipped together but can be separated if one partner becomes ill.

BEDS UPDATE

2

Most of our customers are looking for a mattress which is comfortable and supportive. This will be different for everyone, since a person's height and build will determine which style is most suitable. The majority of our customers opt for a firm mattress.

The term 'orthopaedic' means extra firm and these may be too hard for some people. Foam mattresses are non-allergenic and do not need turning.

CHOOSING YOUR NEW BED

Our Progress showrooms stock a range of beds that can make a big difference to the quality of your sleep.

We recommend that our customers lie on a selection of beds in the showroom to compare comfort and support. If you share your bed, try out the beds together.

Look for a firm core support. This will hold your spine in correct alignment. A quilted surface will give better insulation.

BEDS UPDATE

3

TAKING CARE OF YOUR BED

A new bed is not a cheap purchase. It makes sense to keep your bed in good condition. In this way, it will last and be comfortable throughout its lifetime.

Use a protective cover on your mattress and pillows. Some covers protect against allergies. Vacuum your mattress and base occasionally to remove dust. Air your bed every day so that perspiration can evaporate and the bed stays fresh.

Careful attention to your sleeping habits can result in much improved rest.

BEDS UPDATE

WORD PROCESSING EXERCISE WP 2.5: WORKED EXAMPLE

HOT AIR BALLOONS

Ballooning is an activity that has inspired people to test their endurance and capabilities to the limit. The first crossing of the English Channel was undertaken by a Frenchman and his American co-pilot and actually took place as long ago as 1785. During the early and middle parts of the last century, balloonists concentrated on setting altitude records.

In 1935 a new altitude record was set which remained unchallenged for 20 years. The balloon reached a height of 72,395 feet or 13.7 miles. The success of the attempt showed that humans could survive in a pressurised chamber at this high altitude. It provided invaluable data that was used in future space travel.

The quest for attaining the altitude record was followed by balloonists concentrating on distance and flight duration times. The Atlantic Ocean was crossed successfully followed a few years later by flights across the Pacific Ocean.

PROGRESS BALLOONS

2

There have been several famous people who have taken part in these challenges. Their exploits seem to fire the public's imagination and their progress is watched avidly. Ballooning is an activity that has inspired people to test their endurance and capabilities to the limit.

The main parts of a balloon are the basket, envelope and burner.

The basket of a hot air balloon carries the passengers, pilot and gas cylinders. It is made of woven cane which is fairly light in weight but at the same time is flexible and sturdy. This strength is needed as it has to withstand considerable force on landing.

3

There are two main types of basket. One is designed with compartments

so that passengers can be separated from the pilot and cylinders. The

other one has no compartments so the passengers, pilot and cylinders are

all housed together. The compartments allow the weight to be distributed

evenly and this improves safety.

The envelope is the actual balloon. The main part is made from the same
material used for parachutes. It is a combination of nylon and polyester.
Nylon is a reliable material because it is lightweight, strong and has a high
melting temperature. The bottom part of the envelope is made from a
flame resistant material.

The burner propels the hot air up into the envelope so that the balloon can

take off. Hot air balloons are based on the basic principle that hot air rises

in cooler air. Propane gas is used in modern balloons. It is highly

compressed in cylinders and flows to the burner in liquid form.

Companies frequently decide to use hot air balloons to advertise their

products or services. It can be an effective form of advertising. The

balloon can be made in a variety of shapes, sizes and colours.

PROGRESS BALLOONS

WORD PROCESSING EXERCISE WP 2.6: WORKED EXAMPLE

Greenhouse Information

ADVICE ON CHOOSING A GREENHOUSE

You need to consider what you are going to use the greenhouse for. They can be used for propagating seeds and plants. They allow the gardener to extend the growing season so enabling you to grow flowers and vegetables earlier in the year.

The general advice has been that you will always need a larger greenhouse than you think you need.

SHAPE

Generally modern greenhouses can be divided into 4 shapes. There is the lean-to. This is where one wall is formed by the house or other building and the greenhouse leans on this wall. Unlike conservatories there is often no direct access to the house. They do not suffer from temperature extremes because of the wall. Usually it is easier to get electricity and water services to the lean-to.

The other common type is the apex. This is freestanding and has a pitched roof with parallel sides. The Dutch light greenhouse has sloping sides and the hexagonal type has angular sides.

2

Greenhouse Information

TYPE

The choice is usually between timber and aluminium with new materials being developed. There are a variety of different types of timber such as pine, cedar, teak and oak. A range of timber may be used within the same greenhouse. Aluminium greenhouses require no maintenance. They do not rust. They are cheaper than timber but do not look as attractive. If the bolts and screws are made of steel these may corrode. Timber greenhouses need to be repainted regularly. Alternatives such as polyethylene and acrylic are cheaper but short lived.

HEATING

Heating is expensive. Think about whether it is necessary to heat the whole of the greenhouse or only part of it. An alternative to heating is to have a heated propagator or propagators. This would require electrical sockets. Another option might be to have a very small heated greenhouse and a separate polytunnel.

3

Greenhouse Information

SIZE

You need to consider what you are going to use the greenhouse for.

Having decided on this, to help you choose a suitable size, lay out each activity on your lawn. For example, if you want to grow tomatoes, put out the grow-bags required. Remember to leave space down the middle for the walkway. It is usually better to have a wider greenhouse than a longer one as there will be less walkway and more growing space.

GLAZING

There is a wide range such as horticultural glass, toughened glass or plastic glazing. Think about whether you need automatic vents. A closed greenhouse may heat up to tropical temperatures during the day.

Time spent doing research before buying a greenhouse is time well spent.

WORD PROCESSING EXERCISE WP 2.7: WORKED EXAMPLE

WALKING IN THE SWISS ALPS

Our next planned excursion will take place in June. We propose to travel <u>by luxury coach</u> to Switzerland. We will stay in a 4-star hotel in the beautiful town of Interlaken. From there we will arrange trips into the mountains. We will also organise walks in the foothills for those who are fit.

If you prefer not to walk, there are open air spas where you can swim or relax in the warm sunshine. The excursion will last for nine days.

The cost of £350 includes seven nights' accommodation in Interlaken and one overnight stop in France on the outgoing and return journeys.

If you would like to reserve your place, please let us have details of your

Name and address
Nationality
Passport
Phone number (mobile)
Travelling companion

as soon as possible.

A deposit of £100 per person will also be required.

Places are limited so don't delay. Book your place today!

157

VOLUNTEERING AT LOWER MIDDLETON PRIMARY SCHOOL

As many of you know the Partnership Fund runs a gardening project with Lower Middleton Primary School.

In time it is hoped to extend this project to other local primary schools.

 A range of easy to grow varieties are needed which can be sown at different times of the year. To kick start the project if anyone has spare vegetable seeds please pass these on to Jill Bacon.

We particularly need seeds of:

Cabbages
Courgettes
Leeks
Lettuces
Peas
Potatoes
Radishes

Come and meet other volunteers and find out more about the volunteering projects at the open evening which is being held on 26 October from 5.30pm in the canteen.

Over 50 people volunteer on a regular basis. If you have little spare time, what about volunteering for our 2 big fundraising days in June and September?

Remember any money that is raised by the Partnership Fund is matched by the company.

157

BALLOON FLIGHTS

Experience the magic of a ride in a hot air balloon. Nothing can compare with floating gently over undulating countryside. Familiar landmarks look so different when viewed from above.

Celebrate in style. Come with friends to share in this unique experience.

Where will your flight end? The destination is dictated solely by wind direction and speed.

The items listed will contribute to a comfortable and memorable flight.

Batteries for camera
Binoculars
Camcorder
Camera
Flat footwear
Fleece
Sunglasses
Warm clothing

The flight will last for around one hour. Be prepared that the landing may be bumpy. Our pilot will ensure that discomfort is kept to a minimum. Passengers will be transported back to the starting point. Finish your special day with a celebratory glass of champagne!

Progress Balloons undertakes to do everything possible to ensure that flights take place as scheduled. Adverse weather conditions may necessitate the cancellation of flights at short notice.

153 words

WORD PROCESSING EXERCISE WP 2.10: WORKED EXAMPLE

CLEAN YOUR HOUSE THE PROGRESS WAY!

If you are too busy to spend time cleaning your home, why not take a break and give Progress Cleaning Services a call? Our professional staff can visit <u>weekly or monthly</u> and will clean your house to an exceptional standard. Book online at www.progresscleaning.co.uk.

Our normal schedule includes the following services:

Clean soft furnishings
Clear away rubbish
Dust all surfaces
Polish mirrors
Vacuum carpets
Wash floors
Wipe down paintwork

However, should you wish us to concentrate on a particular room or perform an intensive
clean, we can undertake specific tasks. We charge by the hour and you can limit the time
we spend in your home.

So why not make a booking today?

For a limited period only, we are delighted to offer new customers a 10% discount on their first booking.

Please email us if you would like to receive our informative booklet. Get in touch today.

150

PROGRESS SANDWICH BAR

We have established our reputation by using the best quality ingredients. We guarantee to provide the freshest sandwiches, rolls and baguettes.

Our bread is traditionally baked each day. We use free range eggs, vegetables and salad from our own smallholding. Our meat is supplied by a local farmer. All our suppliers are reputable.

We offer an extensive and imaginative choice of breads and fillings. Tell us if you want something different. We can <u>mix and match</u> our ingredients to meet your requirements.

Here is a selection of items available daily.

Cheese flans
Crisps and dips
Nourishing soups
Sandwiches and baguettes
Sausage rolls
Traditional cakes
Tropical fruit platter

Fruit such as apples, oranges and bananas can be purchased individually. For those with a sweet tooth, taste our mouth-watering pastries and desserts.

Our new sandwich bar opens next Monday in Old Square.

Telephone or fax 01884 66147 with your order and claim an introductory 20% discount.

157 words

WORD PROCESSING EXERCISE WP 2.12: WORKED EXAMPLE

FROM FEBRUARY 1 TO JULY 1 AT THE RIVER FIELD SHOWGROUND

(Turn left at the Beechwood traffic lights. There is plenty of parking at the end of the field.)

There will be a permanent display of over 20 of the latest greenhouses.

Consultants from Green Greenhouses will be available to offer advice on selecting the appropriate greenhouse.

 The range includes contemporary designs. There are timber and aluminium greenhouses which are available in a wide range of sizes and shapes. A new <u>hexagonal design</u> is proving popular as it has very attractive features at a competitive price.

The majority of greenhouses have a choice of glazing from toughened or horticultural glass. There is the option to purchase automatic vents.

A range of chicken coops will also be on display.

The following greenhouse accessories will be on offer at a 25% discount.

Electric propagators
Guttering
Heaters
Horticultural fleece
Seed trays
Slatted staging
Solid staging
Watering cans

154

WORD PROCESSING EXERCISE WP 2.13: WORKED EXAMPLE

PROGRESS HOLIDAYS

In times of financial uncertainty, people look for ways to reduce costs, particularly at holiday times. If you have been worried about the costs of hiring holiday accommodation overseas, the following table will convince you that it is cheaper than you thought!

BOOKING OPTIONS	BOOKING CODE	PRE-BOOKING REQUIRED?	COST PER WEEK £
BUDGET APARTMENT ON COSTA DEL SOL			
Apartment to sleep 4 people	APC1	Yes	276.00
Rental vehicle (4 days)	HCA9	No	89.70
Regular cleaning service	DCS3	No	75.50
Welcome food pack	WFP5	Yes	25.90
Use of beach hut	UBH2	No	20.00
LUXURY VILLA ON COSTA DEL SOL			
Secluded villa to sleep 4 people	VAH1	Yes	960.00
Daily housekeeper	DHK6	Yes	240.00
Membership of health club	MMC8	No	100.00
Rental vehicle (4 days)	HCA9	No	89.70

The above prices include local taxes. All Progress properties enjoy the use of a pool and barbecue.

A 10% reduction is available for new customers.

QUALITY FARE FROM PROGRESS

New sandwich recipes are being introduced in a selection of our stores. Our website www.progress.fare.co.uk gives full details of the location of these trial stores. Download a sample menu.

BREAD	CHOICE OF FILLING	COST AND AVAILABILITY	
		RETAIL PRICE £	LOCATION OF STORE

ASSORTED SANDWICH SELECTION

Ciabatta	Chargrilled vegetables	2.65	Taunton
Farmhouse	Mozzarella cheese with tomato and basil	2.70	Exeter
Wholemeal	Cream cheese with roasted vegetables	2.95	Taunton
Wheatmeal	Bacon, lettuce and sun-dried tomatoes	3.25	Yeovil
Wheatmeal	Roast lamb with organic mint jelly	3.75	Bristol
Pitta	Steak with spicy horseradish relish	3.90	Bath
Granary	Chicken breast with herbs and chutney	3.95	Bath

SPECIALITY SANDWICH PLATTERS

Wheat-free	Selection of tasty regional cheeses	13.95	Chard
Farmhouse	Chicken and turkey with coriander salad	15.75	Bristol
Granary	Scottish smoked salmon, prawns and tuna	16.50	Barnstaple

Telephone 01404 747033 with your order. Take advantage of our daily delivery service straight to your door.

WORD PROCESSING EXERCISE WP 2.15: WORKED EXAMPLE

NEW PRODUCTS

The latest catalogue will be available by the end of next month. You will see from the sample items listed below that our range is expanding into fruit and vegetables.

DESCRIPTION	SIZE	CODE AND WHOLESALE PRICE	
		STOCK NUMBER	PRICE (£)
ORNAMENTAL GARDEN FEATURES			
Victorian bell jar	Medium	VB7	25.50
Willow obelisk	150 cm high	WW5	40.50
Obelisk pyramid	180 cm high	PP2	100.00
Pyramid cold frame	120 cm square	CF24	150.00
Decorative fruit cage	250 cm square	FC9	390.00
GARDENING ACCESSORIES			
Vegetable planters	45 cm diameter	PP6	5.00
Insulating fleece	1000 cm long	FL7	9.25
Strawberry tower	Holds 24	ST3	26.00
Micromesh tunnel cloche	90 cm long	BP2	30.00
Aluminium fruit cage	90 cm high	FC8	105.00

Josie Holland is handling all suppliers' enquiries. She is sending out the catalogue to all our registered suppliers. If you do not receive it by the beginning of August or need any other help please ring her on 024 7647 0033.

FELINE FANCIES
Hillside House
LUTTERWORTH
LE24 6TP

0116 234 7652

Our ref JM/SHL

Day Month Year

Mrs S Hollings
48 Windsor Street
OADBY
LE9 4MP

Dear Mrs Hollings

Thank you for your letter asking about the facilities on offer at our boarding cattery. I note that you have two elderly cats that will need daily grooming.

We set up Feline Fancies over ten years ago. We can accommodate up to 50 cats at any one time. We live in the adjoining house so you can be sure that your pets are always in safe hands. Our business is open all year round and our reputation has grown mainly through word of mouth. Our superb facilities include

- modern accommodation blocks with plenty of room for the cats to exercise in their own run
- heated beds and underfloor heating in the runs during the winter months
- home pickup and drop-off service at no extra charge.

We also offer reduced rates for regular customers. If you decide to bring your cats to board with us, it is vital that you

- ensure that each cat has received flea and worming treatments in the week prior to arrival
- bring the current vaccination certificates with you
- take out insurance against accident and illness
- leave us a contact telephone number so that we can contact you in an emergency.

2

We recommend that all potential customers visit our cattery before boarding their pets with us. To make an appointment, please contact me on the above number.

I look forward to welcoming you to Feline Fancies in the very near future.

Yours sincerely

Judy McNabb
Proprietor

Copies to

Helen Martin
File

PROGRESS BANK SERVICES

Progress House
Westwood Way
Coventry
Warwickshire
CV4 8BR

Telephone 024 7647 0033

Our ref CH/1709/na

1 February 2009

Miss Olivia Osbourn
1400 Alabaster Avenue
ILFRACOMBE
Devon
EX34 6SS

Dear Miss Osbourn

I confirm that your application to open a current account with us has been approved. You will be receiving an introductory pack which should reach you within five working days. The pack will give you comprehensive information on how to run your account.

We list below some reasons why opening an account with us will be beneficial to you.

- **You can access your account 24 hours a day.**
- We can arrange for direct debits to be paid from your account.
- We have a wide range of accessible branches.

We are introducing new measures which are designed to combat fraud. Our staff may ask you to provide additional identification or will contact you to confirm instructions. We would ask you to be patient with these security measures. They are in place solely for your protection.

Page 2

In the meantime, there are various steps that you can take to avoid becoming a victim of fraudulent practices.

- Memorise your Personal Identification Number. Do not disclose it to anyone else. Notify us promptly if you suspect that a third party has obtained access to this number.
- Do not provide personal details to anyone over the telephone.
- Keep your bank account details confidential.

Please be vigilant at all times and check your bank and card statements regularly. You should advise us immediately if you notice any unfamiliar transactions.

Do not hesitate to contact me if you need further information.

Yours sincerely

Carol Hoad
Account Manager

Copy: Gabriel Gray
        Files

WORD PROCESSING EXERCISE WP 2.18: WORKED EXAMPLE

THE PARTNERSHIP FUND
Sector Maintenance Ltd
Sector House
Pit Street
SHEFFIELD
S1 3XX

Telephone 0114 486490   Fax 0114 486491

Our Ref NJ240

Date of Task

Mr J Hudson
Useful Greenhouses Ltd
Unit 8
Pine Street
SHEFFIELD
S17 9YU

Dear Mr Hudson

Further to our site meeting and very useful telephone call I am writing to confirm the points we agreed yesterday. I will arrange for the contractor to

- take down and remove the existing shed and foundations from the site
- build new foundations, including a water channel for drainage, to the measurements provided by your company in the quotation
- put in an electricity supply and connect it after the greenhouse has been constructed.

Your company will

- deliver the greenhouse and take away all the packaging
- erect the greenhouse to the agreed specification and ensure that there is easy access for the electricity supply
- provide all the staging.

In return for your generous gift of the staging Pip North has agreed that this will be shown in the school publicity over the greenhouse. She is arranging for an official opening to take place and hopes that you will be able to attend.

We are very grateful for all your help and guidance. It is much appreciated both by us and the school and hopefully this greenhouse will prove a success with the children. As well as giving them enjoyment it will provide the school with a useful learning resource.

Our Partnership Fund supports 5 primary schools in the district. It is anticipated that within 2 years we can offer greenhouses to all the schools if this one is successful.

Yours sincerely

Jill Bacon
Fund Co-ordinator

cc Pip North
File

WORD PROCESSING EXAM WP 2.A: WORKED EXAMPLE

WELLBEING

FITNESS

With today's sedentary lifestyle, regular exercise should become part of your daily routine. Young and old alike can follow a fitness programme. The guidelines suggest 30 minutes per day for an adult but this can be split into 3 sessions, each of 10 minutes. Some people will find this much easier to sustain.

Exercise does not have to take place in a gym. Walking to the shops, for example, will count as part of your fitness programme. Try getting off the bus one stop before you normally do and walk that extra distance to your home.

You should always use the stairs instead of a lift or escalator. Put this into practice whilst shopping, at railway stations or in multi-storey car parks.

WELLBEING

Some cycle paths also provide interesting and varied places to walk. If you are near a canal, walk along the bank. You will benefit from the exercise and can see all kinds of wildlife at the same time.

Exercise is an important part of a healthy life. It improves fitness and mental awareness. It is a contributory factor in maintaining a healthy weight whilst avoiding the dangers of obesity. Remember that by adopting a healthy lifestyle, you can set an example to your children or grandchildren.

Combine moderate exercise with more energetic activities to create a proper balance. Take up new leisure interests that involve exertion of some kind. These could include gardening, swimming, cycling and home decorating.

Once regular exercise has been introduced into your daily routine, it is essential to stay motivated. Keep reminding yourself of the reasons for starting your fitness programme. Chemicals and hormones released in the brain during exercise help to reduce stress levels. On a cold, wet day when you would rather not go out for your brisk walk, remind yourself of how much better you will feel afterwards.

2

WELLBEING

Set yourself achievable objectives. This will convince you that you are making steady progress towards your ultimate goal.

The time spent exercising is never wasted. Use the quality time to escape problems or worries whilst improving your fitness and wellbeing.

Exercise is especially good for elderly people. It is important that they should retain their mobility as much as possible. Walking and gardening are two activities that will improve co-ordination and balance whilst strengthening muscles.

Remember that by adopting a healthy lifestyle, you can set an example to your children or grandchildren. Children often go to school by car and have very little daily physical activity outside playtime at school. Young people need at least 60 minutes of moderate exertion each day. A high proportion of this time should be devoted to exercise that strengthens bones and muscles and increases flexibility.

3

PROGRESS FITNESS CLUB

OPEN DAY

Do you want a healthier lifestyle? Do you need to lose weight and tone up flabby muscles? Do you want to improve your general wellbeing?

Let us help you to achieve these goals. Start to change your life for the better.

Come along and see what our club can offer.

Cross country running
Cycling
Gym
Swimming
Walking
Water sports
Weight training

Experienced trainers are on hand to give advice and guidance on the best programme for you. Meet like-minded people who want to improve their fitness.

Start with an easy programme. Gently increase to more strenuous exertion. Once you have had the chance to try some of the activities, we hope you will decide to become a member of our club.

We have a limited number of vacancies. We are looking for enthusiastic members who will take advantage of all our facilities.

Contact our secretary on 01809 681481 for full details.

156 words

4

PROGRESS BOUQUETS

We have recently introduced a new online service that supplies quality goods and a range of special offers at affordable prices. We pride ourselves on providing the best value for money.

DESCRIPTION	OFFER	DETAILS FOR ORDERING	
		ITEM NUMBER	SPECIAL PRICE £
SPECIAL OCCASIONS AND DIAMOND COLLECTION			
Oriental lilies with roses	Free wine	SDC45	39.99
Gerbera and chrysanthemums	Luxury wrap	SDC47	32.95
Luxury cream roses	Crystal bowl	SDC54	29.99
Fragrant lilac, freesia and roses	Glass vase	SDC42	27.75
Mixed carnations with statice	Liqueur truffles	SDC49	25.00
BUDGET SELECTION OF FLOWERS AND PLANTS			
Elegant purple orchid	Ceramic pot	BFP24	16.99
Hand-tied button chrysanthemums	Textured sleeve	BFP22	15.99
Fragrant climbing jasmine	Terracotta pot	BFP36	14.99
Fuchsia spray carnations	Plain vase	BFP35	11.99
Mixed single carnations	Free postage	BFP21	9.99

We have been established for over 20 years. We cater for all occasions. We guarantee that our flowers will remain fresh for at least 10 days.

PROGRESS DEALS PLC

Progress House
Westwood Way
Coventry
Warwickshire
CV4 8BR

Telephone 024 7647 0033

Our ref CP/VS/CC

28 January 2009

Miss C Carr
44 Market Square
SALCOMBE
TQ8 2BB

Dear Miss Carr

Thank you for your letter. I confirm that your request to convert your token points to vouchers is receiving our attention. These vouchers can be exchanged for goods or services at any of the participating businesses listed in our brochure.

Some popular choices are given below.

- Book a holiday or short break from the wide selection on offer.
- Treat yourself to a night at the theatre and one night's luxury accommodation.
- Choose from a range of leisure activities or club membership deals.

Visit our website at www.progressdeals.co.uk for full details of the terms and conditions relating to the implementation of this voucher scheme.

Page 2

Please be aware that certain conditions apply when exchanging vouchers.

- Only you as the named holder may use these vouchers.
- The vouchers cannot be used in conjunction with any other special promotion.
- Your vouchers can be topped up with cash but no change will be given if the value of the vouchers exceeds the total cost of goods purchased.

Our vouchers are only valid for a period of six months. Regrettably, there is no facility to renew them so you should ensure that they are exchanged for goods or services before the expiry date.

Your vouchers will be dispatched to you today and should reach you within two working days. Telephone our Customer Services staff on 0800 470033, quoting your reference number 8611680, if you have any queries.

Yours sincerely

Claire Pidgeon
Voucher Scheme Manager

Copy: Florence McDougall
        Files

WORD PROCESSING EXAM WP 2.B: WORKED EXAMPLE

LIGHTING YOUR HOME

LIGHTING YOUR HOME

Changing your lighting is important either when decorating a new room or remodelling an old one. It can be a cheap way of modernising your home. It has the power not only to give you the light source you need for everyday activities but to add to your home a variety of moods. Our lighting consultants are available to help with any questions you may have.

It is easy to become overwhelmed by the different designs that are available. Do not put in new lighting or a new decorative lamp to then find that it does not fit in with your existing decoration. Check the room for any electrical sockets before you buy a new decorative lamp. Utilise the new lighting to enhance your existing furniture and décor. Take your time to do some research.

Do not rely on natural light from your windows to provide all your lighting. It is surprising how often you need extra light, especially in a kitchen, even in the middle of the day.

LIGHTING INFORMATION

Adding an extra decorative lamp is often not a feasible option in some rooms such as bathrooms or kitchens.

Think about the mood you want to convey from your lighting. Then think about whether the function of the light is for general lighting, task lighting or accent lighting.

For general lighting purposes, whatever the room, recessed lighting seems popular. It gives a relaxed atmosphere and is useful if there is limited space.

The next function of interior lighting is task lighting. Task lighting is known to provide lighting for household duties such as cooking, cleaning, reading and working.

Last but not least there is accent lighting. Accent lighting is designed to brighten up a particular feature. This could be a picture or an architectural feature. It is an easy way of updating your home.

2

LIGHTING INFORMATION

KITCHEN LIGHTING

Ceiling lighting can be important in a kitchen because there are so many different needs. The kitchen is often the busiest part of the house. As a great source of light consider using fluorescent fixtures which will also help save on energy bills. Downlighters mounted off the edge of cabinets are an excellent way to create additional lighting.

To help prevent shadows on the worktops consider the use of lights under cabinets. In open areas such as over sinks, use recessed downlighters mounted directly over the sink. Illuminate particular areas such as any architectural detail or eating areas with recessed or track lighting. Directional lighting will cast light on just the right places in your kitchen.

Our lighting consultants are available to help with any questions you may have.

3

LOW VOLTAGE LIGHTING

These lights always stay cool and can be used safely in close proximity to furnishings.

Each light comes with a health and safety leaflet.

They are <u>safe with children</u> and are more reliable than traditional fairy lights and are cheaper to run. In the home, if used imaginatively, they can create wonderful features. Indoor and outdoor lights are available.

Their traditional use was at Christmas but more and more people are using them all the year round.

Our most popular lights include:

Cherry blossom tree
Christmas tree
Curtains
Fairy
Flowers
Icicles
Nets
Ropes

To give you fresh ideas on how they can be used come and see our display at the Lighting Exhibition between 3 and 16 October at the New Town Hall, Stoke Street.

Every weekend there will be a permanent display at The Malthouse.

Visit our website at <u>www.maltlights.co.uk</u> to see our latest product range and place an order.

154

LIGHTS ON OFFER

The following lights are some of the lines now on offer at a substantial discount. These are end of lines and none of the stock is faulty in any way. All purchases come with a 2-year guarantee and a health and safety leaflet.

DESCRIPTION	CODE	CONCESSIONARY PRICES	
		COST (£) INCLUDING VAT	PERCENTAGE DISCOUNT
CHRISTMAS AND SPECIAL OCCASIONS			
Waterfall with star	WS2	79.95	50
Illuminated tree	TT6	59.00	30
Christmas conifer	CC23	36.00	22
White and blue icicles	WB9	9.35	18
AVAILABLE ALL THE YEAR ROUND			
Red pyracantha	RP6	9.50	50
Blue and white battery	BB3	4.55	37
Magenta nets	MN8	25.50	35
Butterfly (pink or white)	PB7	14.50	25
Connectable rope	CR5	19.95	24
Lavender curtains	LC2	30.00	20

Offers are changed on a regular basis. Visit our website at www.maltlights.co.uk to see our latest product range and to place an order. Availability is dependent on our suppliers.

USEFUL GREENHOUSES LTD

Unit 8
Pine Street
SHEFFIELD   Telephone 0114 348756
S17 9YU   Fax 0114 348757

Our Ref JH/345

Date of exam

Mrs Nadia Jones
78 Fell Road
SHEFFIELD
S17 4JK

Dear Mrs Jones

Thank you for your queries about buying one of our greenhouses. I agree that it is difficult to choose from so many styles and sizes.

If you decide to buy one of our greenhouses we will free of charge

- come and do a site visit and measure the area where you envisage the greenhouse will stand
- give advice on the different types of greenhouses which may be suitable for your site and requirements
- include a free information sheet on choosing a greenhouse.

For buildings over £5000 we will do all the construction work. This includes

- taking down any existing structures
- putting in any foundations and constructing the building
- carrying out all electrical work including lighting and power points and also doing any plumbing work.

Individual quotations are given for each type of work. This helps you choose the service you require us to do.

It may help you to decide on the size and type of greenhouse if you come and see our display of timber and aluminium structures. This is being held at River Field Showground from 1 February to 1 July. There are over 20 greenhouses of different designs on show and also a display of equipment such as staging, propagators and smaller items such as soft horticultural fleece. A consultant is always on site to offer advice.

Please contact me if you need any further advice.

Yours sincerely

Jon Hudson
Sales Manager

cc Kate Mosto
File

2

WORD PROCESSING EXAM WP 2.C: WORKED EXAMPLE

INFORMATION SHEET

PROGRESS PROPERTIES

Progress Properties started in business almost 15 years ago and we now enjoy international recognition.   Last year we won the coveted Builder of the Year Award. We are particularly well-known for the quality of our properties and our attention to the environment. Read on to see why you can trust Progress.

When you choose a Progress home you can rest assured that you are in safe hands.

NEW DEVELOPMENTS

There are currently 120 developments in progress across the UK and mainland Europe. These range from modern estates of 100 plots to small apartment developments. For your closest new build, log on to our website. There you will find a location map, a site plan and a description of the properties, along with their prices.

ECO-FRIENDLY OPTIONS

Some of our newest builds include properties with a full range of eco-friendly options. These include solar panels for low cost heating and triple insulation of floors and walls.

Some of our properties also have the option of rooftop planting. This offers a rainwater harvesting system which collects water. The water can be used in flushing toilets.

We can also offer automatic shutters to stop the properties getting too hot in the summer months.

INFORMATION SHEET

PART-EXCHANGE SCHEME

In the current climate, it is often quite difficult to sell your home at a reasonable price. That is why we offer our part-exchange scheme. Under this scheme, we value your property and offer you the current market value. All you have to do is find the difference between the cost of your property and the price of your new Progress home. We do all the paperwork.

Contracts can be exchanged within four weeks. For a stress-free move, please check out our website for full details of how to make an application. It really could not be easier.

FIRST TIME BUYERS

Most of our new developments include properties designed to appeal to the first time buyer. Not only do they offer modern, open plan living spaces, they are also fully equipped with kitchen appliances and basic lounge and bedroom furniture. Again, this makes for a simple move without all the additional costs involved in fitting out a new home.

2

INFORMATION SHEET

CONTACT US

If you would like more information about any of our developments or if you wish to speak to a member of our sales team, please get in touch. Our telephone number is 024 7647 0033. Our lines are open from 10 am until 5 pm every day. We look forward to hearing from you.

When you choose a Progress home you can rest assured that you are in safe hands.

Stop Press! We have some fantastic properties which have been reduced by 30%. Call us for details of these brilliant deals!

3

PROPERTIES TO RENT

If you are wondering where to spend your holiday this year, why not consider joining us at The Haven, our new development on the edge of Lake Marvel?

 This apartment complex comprises properties for purchase and rental. There is a health club, pub and convenience store on site. Located only 5 minutes' walk from the lake, The Haven is an ideal holiday choice.

The apartments offer identical accommodation. An open-plan sitting room adjoins a well-equipped kitchen. The double bedrooms have queen-sized beds and large fitted wardrobes. The luxury bathroom has a separate shower and a whirlpool bath. Rental prices start at £250 per week in the low season.

Each rental property offers these facilities as standard:

Audio system
Automatic washing machine
Dishwasher
Television and DVD
Towels and bedlinen
Underfloor heating

Our larger properties have attractive terraces with a barbecue area.

Fuel and power costs are included in the rental price.

PROGRESS PROPERTIES – LIVE THE DREAM!

158

THE COST OF BUYING YOUR NEW HOME

The following table outlines the costs involved in the purchase of a new home. These expenses can add up to £4,000 to the purchase price. This can come as an unpleasant surprise for the inexperienced buyer. If you buy a Progress property, these expenses are forgotten because our prices are all-inclusive!

ITEM OF EXPENDITURE	ITEM CODE	FURTHER DETAILS	
		OPTIONAL EXPENSE?	APPROX COST £
EXPENSES INCURRED PRIOR TO PURCHASE			
Solicitors' fees (basic service)	E23	No	750.00
Mortgage arrangement fee	E25	No	400.00
Property survey (basic)	E51	No	350.00
Money transfer fee	E26	No	25.50
Bankruptcy search	E17	No	7.50
POSSIBLE COSTS INCURRED AFTER PURCHASE			
Television and DVD player	F14	Yes	495.00
Oven, hob and microwave	F78	Yes	350.00
Washing machine	F74	Yes	250.00
Refrigerator and freezer	F72	Yes	200.00

The above costs are based upon a property valued at £200,000. They do not include stamp duty.

PROGRESS PROPERTIES
Construction House
Danvers Lane
COVENTRY
CV3 9JH

024 7647 0033

Our ref JL/ENQ

Day Month Year

Mr and Mrs H Fretwell
65 Nelson Road
BANBURY
OX16 3DM

Dear Mr and Mrs Fretwell

Thank you for your recent enquiry about our new building developments in the West Midlands. We are pleased to inform you that we are just finishing some new townhouses on the outskirts of Leamington Spa. I enclose a brochure giving details of the homes and their exact location.

When you have studied the brochure, please contact me if you would like to arrange a guided viewing. There has been much interest in these properties. I would therefore urge you not to wait too long before making a decision.

This particular development offers

- a fantastic location close to a range of shopping and leisure options
- spacious accommodation finished to the highest quality and with a fully-fitted kitchen
- one guaranteed car parking space
- an opportunity to negotiate a part-exchange deal on your current home

These homes are eco-friendly. The solar thermal panels in the roof generate hot water, the properties are triple glazed and floors and walls alike are well insulated.

What is more, all Progress properties benefit from

- special deals for first time buyers
- a ten-year builders' warranty
- great rates on home and contents insurance premiums
- attractive landscaped gardens for outdoor dining and well-maintained communal grounds

2

Prices range from £175,000 to under £350,000.

Progress will be delighted to offer you a substantial discount if you sign a preliminary agreement by the end of the month.

I look forward to hearing from you.

Yours sincerely

Jed Lowe
Marketing Executive

Copies

Mark Wilson
File

AUDIO-TRANSCRIPTION EXERCISE AT 2.1: WORKED EXAMPLE

DOCUMENT 1 – worked example

Progress Group
Westwood Way
COVENTRY
CV4 8JQ

024 7647 0033

Our Ref GR/RJ

16 January 2009

FIRST CLASS

Mrs Sara Crowe
18 Village Way
CROYDON
CR4 8AF

Dear Mrs Crowe

<u>Progress Cottage Holidays</u>

It has been some time since you had a Progress holiday so I have pleasure in enclosing our latest brochure. I hope this will remind you of the wide choice, vast range of destinations and superb value we offer.

At Progress we have always believed in looking after the pennies on your behalf. This year we have managed to maintain the two things which make us so popular: wide choice and maximum affordability. As a result you can now take a Progress break from less than £7 per person per night. To make budgeting even easier you can now secure your perfect holiday cottage for a special low deposit of only £25. For couples or parties of four or more we offer a discount of 20% off larger properties at off-peak times.

I hope we may have the pleasure of taking your booking in the near future.

Yours sincerely

Geoff Randall
Managing Director

Enc

cc James Vine

Progress Group
Westwood Way
Coventry
CV4 8JQ

024 7647 0033

Our Ref MF/DP

URGENT

24 January 2009

Mrs Amanda Hogan
91 Wessex Drive
GUILDFORD
Surrey
GU3 7JP

Dear Mrs Hogan

Car Insurance

According to our records your car insurance is due for renewal next month. We are sure that we can offer you a better deal than your current insurer. We enclose a leaflet giving some example quotations.

Many people save a great deal of money when they move their car insurance to us. All you need to do is contact us and we will be able to give you a quotation immediately. You will be given a small discount as you have your buildings and contents insurance with us. There are no long forms for you to complete. We can complete the forms for you over the telephone. Our aim is to make the process as fast and as easy as we can for our customers.

We hope you will give us the opportunity to give you a quotation. We look forward to hearing from you in the near future.

Yours sincerely

Mary Farmer
Insurance Manager

Enc

cc   James Roberts
        file

DOCUMENT 1

Progress Group
Westwood Way
COVENTRY
CV4 8JQ

024 7647 0033

Our ref DM/LD

Insert today's date

URGENT

Mrs Helen King
27 Lime Avenue
NORWICH
NN1 8QJ

Dear Mrs King

Catering Equipment

Further to our telephone conversation I confirm that our company can supply all the equipment that is needed to run a small catering business.

I enclose our brochure. We supply products from manufacturers in this country and abroad. We specialise in providing quality goods at affordable prices.

When you have looked at our brochure and know the types and makes of **items you** require just contact me. I will be happy to visit your premises. I could advise you on the best appliances to install in your kitchen.

You will see from the order form that delivery charges are quoted for each item. If you order all of your appliances from us we would be willing to negotiate reduced charges. Unfortunately no guarantee would be given that all items could be delivered on the same day. However, most items usually arrive within ten days of ordering them.

I look forward to hearing from you.

Yours sincerely

Dalton Metcalfe
Sales Manager

Enc

cc James Kelly
    File

MEMORANDUM

To   Maria Delgado

From   Lucinda Parkinson

Date   Day Month Year

Ref   LP/OD

OPEN EVENING

Preparations are well in hand for our open evening next month. The senior leadership team and the careers staff have confirmed that they will be giving presentations. Members of the student support team will also be present to offer advice.

I would like you to organise student volunteers. Their task will be to meet visitors and direct them to the subject area or display that is of particular interest to them. They should also be prepared to answer any questions about the college and the courses we offer.

We need at least two students to be stationed in each of the following areas:

1.   Front entrance
2.   Exhibition hall
3.   Refreshment area

Please remind them that they should dress reasonably smartly. **Jeans will not be allowed.** They must remember that they are ambassadors for the college and their conduct should reflect the high standards we maintain.

MEMORANDUM

To   Daniel Hobson

From   Charles Marshall

Date   24 January 2009

Ref   DH/FW

MONTHLY EXPENSE ACCOUNTS

From next month we are proposing to change the way in which employees claim their expenses. As you know the current procedure is to complete a form and then print it. The employee then attaches the receipts to the form and asks their manager to approve the claim. The form is then taken to the accounts department.

The proposed new procedures are listed below.

1)   Complete the expense claim form as usual.

2)   Scan all the receipts into an electronic file.

3)   Forward both files to the departmental manager.

The claim form will be passed to the accounts department once it has been approved. Employees will have these expenses paid directly into their bank accounts on the tenth working day of each month.

The process will be much faster and more efficient than it is currently.

Please let me know if you have any questions about the new procedures.

DOCUMENT 2

MEMORANDUM

To   Anita Fernandez

From   Bradley Jenkins

Date   Insert today's date

Ref   BJ/GA

DISPLAY REQUIREMENTS

I have managed to get two stands at one of the largest kitchen appliance shows in the country. The largest stand will display appliances. The other stand will have demonstrations of smaller items.

The following arrangements need to be made:

1   Transport to take demonstration units to the venue the day before.

2   Select eight members of staff to be on duty and compile a rota for the day.

3   Hire a minibus to transport all staff attending the event.

I anticipate many people will be interested in the latest range of products we have on offer. I would like two additional staff to demonstrate some of the items that can also be used in the home.

All expenses will be paid. An allowance of £30 will be given for the purchase of refreshments. All receipts must be presented with claim forms otherwise payment will not be made.

DOCUMENT 2 – Advertisement – worked example

TALKING SENSE ABOUT SAVINGS

The financial headlines over the past months have been enough to give anybody sleepless nights. However before you come to the conclusion that you would be better off keeping your money under the mattress talk to us. Our knowledgeable staff are extremely experienced and it is particularly at times like these that this experience counts. **Discussing your savings options with them will help to guarantee that you are doing what is best for your money and your future plans.**

You can contact us in any of the following ways:

1. Drop into your local branch.
2. Visit our website.
3. Call us on 0845 713 1133 between 8.45 am and 5 pm Monday to Friday.

Whichever method you choose you will find our team approachable and helpful. In addition our website has a very informative question and answer section outlining what is happening right now in the economy.

For savings advice you can bank on talk to Progress and sleep soundly.

STAFF VACANCIES

We have recently won a large contract and because of this we need to employ more staff. The new contract starts next month and we therefore require people who can start immediately.

Listed below are the posts currently available.

1)   Typist to work in accounts.

2)   General office clerk in sales.

3)   Secretary to our office manager.

4)   Data entry clerk in marketing.

We will be holding interviews as soon as possible and we will be offering jobs to interviewees on the day.

Only apply if you can start work immediately.

We offer our staff a wide range of benefits. These include free meal vouchers to use in our staff canteen. Our canteen opens early in the morning so that staff can have breakfast before starting work. Hot meals and drinks are served throughout the day.

Please contact Helen Dawson if you would like an application form and further details about any of the above vacancies.

DOCUMENT 2

VACANCY FOR SALES MANAGER

An opening has arisen for a sales manager.   The new post is at our Chester branch.

Application forms are available from the Human Resources Department. All forms must be returned by the end of the month.

All applicants will need to prepare the following information ready for interview.

1   A short presentation showing leadership skills.

2   A proposed plan of action to increase sales.

3   A personal statement giving reasons for interest in the post.

It is planned to invite all applicants for interview. **Please keep your diary free for the first week of next month.**

The successful person will have all of their removal expenses paid for by the company. An allowance towards any bridging loan for the purchase of a house will be given. A company car will be allocated on your appointment.

It is hoped that the successful person will start work in Chester by the end of next month.

DOCUMENT 2 – Notice – worked example

PROGRESS COLLEGE

Progress College has just moved into new premises in Westwood Way. The new building contains suites for music, design and technology and art together with a chapel, offices and general classrooms.

The new facilities will help to enhance the College's reputation for excellence in the arts. As well as a 400 seat auditorium the building also contains:

1.   two drama studios
2.   a dance studio
3.   two music classrooms and five practice rooms
4.   an art suite including a photography workshop.

There will be an open evening in January for prospective students who are thinking of enrolling for a course in September. Please telephone for an invitation. **You will need to bring a parent or guardian with you.** This is because we feel it is important that an adult helps you with the decision about the next stage of your education.

Please note that the event is not suitable for small children.

AUDIO-TRANSCRIPTION EXERCISE AT 2.11: WORKED EXAMPLE

CLOSING DOWN SALE

This store will close at the end of next month and the building will be decorated and modernised. We plan to open again in approximately six months. The majority of the stock will be transported to our store in Swindon but we want to sell some of the stock before we close.

Listed below is some of the merchandise we want to clear.

1)   Clothing for ladies and gentlemen.

2)   Pottery and china tea sets.

3)   Televisions and other electrical items.

4)   Shoes and all kinds of accessories.

As we want to clear the above merchandise we will be reducing prices by at least fifty per cent. There will also be price reductions in many of the other departments in the store.

The sale starts on Monday.

Free tea and coffee will be served in our restaurant on the ground floor. A wide range of hot and cold food will also be available for purchase.

DOCUMENT 2

DANCING CLASSES

This year we have added some new dances to our programme. Ballroom dancing came top in popularity with our members. We have pleasure in introducing the following new classes starting at the beginning of May.

1   Tap dancing for beginners on Thursday evenings starting at 6 pm.

2   Line dancing for all age groups will take place on Friday evenings from 7 pm until 9 pm
     Members will be selected to join the demonstration team.

3   Argentine tango sessions with top dancers. The classes will start at 7 pm and finish at
     9 pm on Monday and Tuesday evenings.

4   Learn to belly dance. This is a one hour session starting at 7 pm on Wednesday evenings.

Do not purchase specialist shoes or clothing at first. Only when you are sure this is the dance you want to continue with should you consider buying footwear and clothing.

Come along and try one of our new classes.

AUDIO-TRANSCRIPTION EXERCISE AT 2.13: WORKED EXAMPLE

DOCUMENT 3 – worked example

ENERGY PERFORMANCE CERTIFICATE

This document is required by law when a building is sold or put up for rent. It rates the energy efficiency of the building from A to G and is valid for ten years.

The table below gives the maximum and minimum levels for each rating:

Rating	Minimum	Maximum
A	92%	100%
B	81%	91%
C	69%	**80%**
D	55%	68%
E	39%	54%
F	21%	38%

Any property with a rating of 20% or below will have very high running costs.

The report will suggest ways of changing the rating of the building and the likely cost savings if these changes are made. You do not have to act on the recommendations contained in the report. However if you decide to do so it could make your home more attractive for sale or rent.

Even if you are not planning to move it might still be worthwhile to apply for a report.

You might find that you can cut your fuel bills if you carry out even some of the suggested improvements.

DOCUMENT 3

EXTRACT FROM SURVEYOR'S REPORT

The preliminary inspection of the cottage and barn at Mayfields Country Estate has now been completed. As agreed a verbal report will be given to the client, Sir Willoughby Duncan-Smythe. If required, a short written report will be produced within ten days.

As a result of the findings it is essential that we present the full outcome of possible costs to the client. The following is a list of the costs that may be involved.

REFERENCE	ITEM	FEES OR COSTS
R1	writing of inspection reports	£800
A2	engage architect	£2,000
T3	employ technical analyst	£1,000
S4	submit schedule of work to be done	£500
R5	carry out remedial work	£300
F6	follow up inspections	£900

The fees will be fixed whereas costs for remedial work may be variable. It is anticipated that the price quoted for the follow up inspections will not increase. After allowing for the above costs and fees consideration will be given to the further progress of the job. The client has to pay all the costs and fees himself. He will then make full claim against his insurance.

PROGRESS COACH TOURS

Progress Coach Tours is pleased to announce that our brochure for next season is now available.

We are increasing the number of destinations for our coach tours. As well as day trips we can now offer a range of touring holidays to customers.

The new touring holidays are listed below.

Tour Reference	Description	Nights
20	Norfolk coastal tour	7
30	Dover Harbour and a boat trip	3
40	Mystery tour	1
50	Brighton and shopping	4
60	London theatre visit	2
70	Tour of the Channel Islands	7

We have selected our hotel accommodation carefully. These hotels are small but clean and comfortable. They provide an excellent choice of food in their restaurants.

All of our coaches are air conditioned and have toilet facilities on board. Each coach has a

kitchen and customers may buy hot and cold drinks during the trip. Some food is also

available.

We can provide cars to collect customers from their homes at the start of their holiday. We can also take them home at the end of the tour. With all holidays costing more than four hundred pounds this service is free.

If you would like a copy of our latest brochure please telephone us.

Progress Group
Westwood Way
Coventry
CV4 8JQ

024 7647 0033

Our Ref KL/BG

FIRST CLASS

17 January 2009

Mr Henry Gupta
5 Hazel Grove
BASINGSTOKE
Hampshire
RG24 9NR

Dear Mr Gupta

Storm Damage

Thank you for returning the claim form giving details of the storm damage to your property.

I enclose a copy of the report written by our inspector. As you can see he says that your garden shed will have to be demolished. Therefore you need to provide us with three estimates for clearing the site and three for replacing the shed.

Although most of the wooden fence panels were blown down some of them are not damaged and can be put back. We have a contract with a company in your area that carries out fence repairs for us. Please obtain an estimate for this work from them. You will find their telephone number in the report.

As this is your first claim the discount on your policy will not change when you renew your insurance. If you have any questions regarding your claim please do not hesitate to contact me.

Yours sincerely

Kathleen Walters
Claims Manager

Enc

cc   Anne Collins
      file

PROGRESS COLLEGE OPEN DAY

We are planning our next open day and we would like as many of our students as possible to be involved. This is to allow prospective students to talk to current students and observe them at work.

Listed below are the main displays and events that we have planned.

1)   Oil painting in the arts and crafts department.

2)   Baking in the home economics department.

3)   The college orchestra will play in the main hall.

4)   Students will give a gymnastic display in the sports centre.

If you would like to volunteer to take part in any of the above you should give your name to Mark Collins. Volunteers are also needed for a variety of other tasks.

Students taking part will be given time to rehearse.

We know that we can rely on all our students for their help and support in this matter and we expect that this open day will be as successful as the last.

DOCUMENT 3

REPORT ON CONTRACTS FOR OFFICE SUPPLIES

The sales figures for last month show a small increase over the previous month. This is very encouraging in the present economic climate.

All the staff in our sales department have worked very hard to win new contracts. As a result we expect a large increase in profits for the year.

The new contracts are as follows:

Contract Number	Items	Weekly Value
10	printer paper	£600
20	ink cartridges	£500
30	brown envelopes	£200
40	pens and pencils	£100
50	coloured folders	£300
60	staples and paper clips	£400

Staff will be told the amount to be distributed through the profit sharing scheme as soon as this has been calculated by the accountants.

For the profit sharing scheme staff will need to have worked for the company for a minimum

of two years in order to qualify. We expect that the amount will be much larger than last

year.

The profit sharing scheme is currently under review. Staff will be notified of any changes as soon as possible.

This business continues to prosper. We owe success to the high standard of our service and the hard work of our staff.

Progress Group
Westwood Way
COVENTRY
CV4 8JQ

024 7647 0033

Our ref MD/PD

30 January 2009

Mr Jeffrey Thornton
19 Purbeck Street
SWINDON
SN2 1AX

FIRST CLASS

Dear Mr Thornton

<u>Motorcycle Insurance</u>

Thank you for choosing Progress again for your motorcycle insurance. Your policy will remain with Acme Insurance. We believe that this company offers the level of cover you need based on the details you have given us.

You may wish to include legal costs, personal accident or breakdown cover. If so they can easily be added to your policy for a small extra cost. Please call us and speak to one of our advisors about this.

The enclosed statement of fact contains all the details you gave us. Your insurance is based on this information and it forms the basis of your contract with your insurer. Please check this document carefully as any errors could mean that you are not insured. If any of your details are wrong or missing please contact us immediately.

In the meantime if you have any questions please do not hesitate to call us.

Yours sincerely

Mike Deakin
Customer Services Manager

Enc

cc Renewals Department

DOCUMENT 2

PROGRESS CONSERVATORIES

With a Progress conservatory you can gain extra space and enjoy your garden all the year round. Our conservatories have all the following features:

1. Superior design and construction.
2. Advanced glass technology.
3. Virtually no maintenance.

If you want a more classic look and feel then choose the natural beauty of timber. **We use only the finest timber for its strength and durability**. It can be worked easily to give you the exact look you want. All our wood is specially treated so that it can breathe naturally. All it needs is an occasional staining or painting and it is guaranteed for thirty years against rot and fungus.

We take care of every step from the initial design and planning consent to installation. We will design your conservatory to your specification or you can choose one of our styles. The most popular are the Victorian and Edwardian.

Call us today on 0800 120 234.

DOCUMENT 3 – worked example

PROGRESS CONFERENCE CENTRE

Progress Conference Centre has been in business for five years. During this time it

has gone from strength to strength. It is now proud to be ranked among the top 100

centres in the country.

The facilities offered are second to none. There are 80 bedrooms with bath and
shower. All have television, a hairdryer and tea and coffee making facilities. A
wireless Internet service is also provided. One room is particularly suitable for a
guest using a wheelchair. It has a wide range of adaptations to make the guest's
stay easier.

The six conference rooms can be laid out in different styles on request. The table

below shows the maximum capacity of each room:

Room	Theatre Style	Boardroom Style
Newport	110	50
Ryde	60	24
Sandown	40	20
Ventnor	40	20
Cowes	30	18
Yarmouth	25	14

For a positive start to the day resident delegates can choose a full English or

Continental breakfast from a self-serve counter. Lunch can be either hot or cold and

always includes at least one vegetarian dish. Soft drinks are served with lunch.

There is ample free car parking on site.

DOCUMENT 1

Progress Group
Westwood Way
COVENTRY
CV4 8JQ

024 7647 0033

Our ref TE/BW

Insert today's date

PERSONAL

Mr Norman Jacques
78 Manor Road
COLWYN BAY
LL28 4XY

Dear Mr Jacques

Computer Upgrade

Thank you for your recent enquiry about our services. There are several ways in which you can improve the capacity and speed of your computer. I enclose a leaflet showing our current offers.

I suggest you give very careful thought as to the economics of upgrading. We have several packages on offer at the moment. I also enclose the new systems leaflet for your information and consideration.

If you decide to go for a complete new system I would be happy to take your old one away. I may be able to make a small allowance against a new system. This would depend on the age and condition of your equipment. I would be prepared to take everything and give it to a charity for passing on to other needy causes.

If I can be of any further help please do not hesitate to contact me or my technical manager on 024 7647 0033.

Yours sincerely

Trevor Eaton
Manager

Encs

cc Mark Stevens
    File

MEMORANDUM

To   Christopher Miller

From   Delia Watson

Date   Insert today's date

Ref   DW/KL

GRAND OPENING

The restaurant is now ready to open.

It is hoped to have the official opening ceremony sometime in April. This will be approximately four weeks after we have opened. This timescale will allow us to sort out any minor teething problems.

The following arrangements need to be made:

1   Ask the chef to compile a suitable menu for 40 guests.

2   Find a local celebrity who is willing to perform the opening.

3   Contact the local press to arrange for a reporter and photographer to attend.

As we have overspent on the budget there is not a lot left to cover the fee of the celebrity. If you can get someone for less than £500 that would be excellent.

The allowance for the food and wine has been increased and is currently eight hundred pounds. **The finest quality must be provided.**

Please keep me informed of developments.

DOCUMENT 3

SELF-CATERING ACCOMMODATION

Progress Holiday Lettings are pleased to announce the acquisition of some new holiday properties.

All of the properties are based in Cornwall. The beach is within ten minutes walking distance. Supermarkets and a variety of small shops are within easy access of local car parking areas.

Bookings will be taken immediately. A deposit is required to secure your booking.

The following list shows some of the new properties where you are able to cater for yourself.

ACCOMMODATION	SLEEPS	PRICE PER WEEK
Converted barn	6 to 8	£650
Cornish cottage	6	£500
Fisherman's cottage	2 to 6	£420
Chalet bungalow	2 to 4	£300
Luxury detached house	6	£550
Stone cottage	2	£400

All of our properties are available for short term or long term rental. Several of our clients book their accommodation for the same weeks each year. Numerous seaside premises are booked at least a year in advance. Check your diary and plan your holiday dates well ahead in order to get your first preference and avoid any disappointment.

Telephone our agency on 024 7647 0033 or visit our website at www.progresslettings.com.